Studies of Capitalist Culture

Studies of Capitalist Culture

By

R. G. Williams

Cambridge
Scholars
Publishing

Studies of Capitalist Culture

By R. G. Williams

This book first published 2023

Cambridge Scholars Publishing

Lady Stephenson Library, Newcastle upon Tyne, NE6 2PA, UK

British Library Cataloguing in Publication Data
A catalogue record for this book is available from the British Library

ISBN (10): 1-5275-1243-6
ISBN (13): 978-1-5275-1243-6

When people speak of the ideas that revolutionise society, they do but express that fact that within the old society the elements of a new one have been created.

—Karl Marx

We must change the world in order to change ourselves.

—Christopher Caudwell

CONTENTS

PREFACE

This book is a study of Capitalist culture. It is a study of modern culture under Capitalism. It is a study of the problems of Capitalist culture. We live in an age of Capitalist crisis. We also live in an age of Capitalist cultural crisis. By looking at the relationship between culture and Capitalism, we might be able to understand the relationship between culture and the struggle for Socialism — for a society based on a free culture and a free humanity.

Culture is how human society expresses its ideas. Culture is how human society develops its ideas. Culture is the process of how human societies create their ideas and preserve them through time and changes in society. Culture is a vital part of humanity. Culture is one of the great achievements of humanity. It allows humanity to remember its ideas — and it allows humanity to express its ideas. The creation of culture, through labour, is a major part of what makes humanity really human. Culture reflects society. Society creates culture. The power of culture is a social power. Indeed, culture has often played a key role in all of the great social revolutions of human history. Culture, as a social force, has often been vital in terms of achieving social progress and social revolution — in the long history of humanity.

This book is an attempt at a Socialist study of culture. Specifically, it is a Socialist study of the politics of culture. This book is a Socialist study. It is a Socialist Humanist study, in the tradition of Democratic Socialism. This book aims to present a Marxist account of the development of culture — of where culture exists in the social struggle for human freedom. It is an attempt to apply the basic ideas of Marx and Engels to the study of culture. It is an attempt to apply the basic ideas of Historical Materialism to the study of culture.

Capitalism, today, has many problems — including cultural problems. The only way to solve these problems is via Socialism.

In order to have a free culture we must build a free society — a Socialist society. Marx was correct in believing that the struggle for Socialism is the struggle for a liberated humanity. We must achieve a Socialist culture and a Socialist society.

R.G. Williams

(2023)

CHAPTER I

CULTURE – A SOCIALIST STUDY

This short essay is a study of culture. It is a Socialist study of what culture is and the social role it plays in society. Today, in the early 21st century, culture is obviously a powerful force in modern human society. Our modern, Capitalist, society is clearly a society being shaped by culture – alongside the other economic, social, and political developments which make up modern society. Culture, today, is obviously a social force – with the power to shape and revolutionise human society. Culture has always been a powerful social force in human history, since the beginning of humanity, but it is also a revolutionary force – helping to drive forward the development of humanity.

Culture is the social expression of social ideas. It is the social development of ideas – through art, literature, and social expression. It is how human societies develop, refine, and shape their ideas. Culture is a social force in human history. It is a revolutionary force in human history – as part of the economic, social, political, and historical revolutions which shape human development. Culture, as part of wider social revolution, can be part of the revolutionary struggle for a better world.1

Culture is how society develops its ideas. Culture, in basic terms, is how any society expresses its ideas. Every society, in human history, has produced its own culture – in order to express its ideas and the social relations of its society. For Socialists, culture is a powerful part of the reality of humanity. Culture is part of what makes human beings really human.

Human beings, collectively, create culture. They create it through their struggle and through their determination to create a better world. Culture only develops by the labour and action of human beings. It is the agency of human beings, and the creative agency of human beings, usually as workers, which pushes forward the development of society.

Culture, like all social forces, is diverse. Culture can be expressed and developed in a variety of ways – through art, literature, film, etc. This diversity of culture allows it to be a varied social force. Culture, at its most revolutionary, has been crucial to the great social revolutions of human history – revolutions which have helped to push forward the struggle for human freedom. Culture, by itself, cannot achieve social progress – as only human beings, and human agency, can achieve social progress – but culture is still vital to understanding and shaping our society. The struggle for a good culture, for a free culture, is a vital part of the struggle for a good and free society. It is a vital part of the struggle for a better society.

Culture belongs to all. Every human being has a right to culture and a right to contribute to the development of culture. Culture is one of the crucial human rights – in any democratic or free society. Culture belongs to everyone. Culture belongs to all. Culture is part of the common heritage of humanity. As Raymond Williams, the great British Socialist, once wrote: 'culture is ordinary … and not elite'.2 This means that culture is part of everyday life, but it also means that culture belongs to ordinary people. Ordinary people can and do contribute to culture – despite what any elitist ruling class might say about culture. Every man, every woman, every child, every nationality, every race, every sex, every gender, every class, and every person, in a good society, deserves culture. Every man, every woman, every child, every nationality, every race, every sex, every gender, every class, and every person can contribute to the development of culture. In order for human beings to live in a free and good society they need to live in a society based on a free culture – on a democratic culture.

For Socialists, culture is one of the great achievements of humanity. Socialists, in political terms, struggle for a society based on the free development of each and the free development of all – e.g. Socialism. This includes the free development of society and the free development of culture. This means that understanding culture, in economic, political, social, historical, and intellectual terms is crucial for the struggle for Socialism – for a free society.

Understanding culture is important. It is important because ideas are important – and culture helps to shape ideas. We are living in a time, at the beginning of the 21st century, where culture is being revolutionised by the social revolutions of our times. If we really wish to understand our times, and the possibilities of our times, we must understand culture – and society.

Culture is clearly political. It is clearly part of the political struggle for a better world. It is obvious, if we look at our society today, that culture is political. This means that the struggle for a free culture is also a political struggle – as is the struggle for a free society. For Socialists, the struggle for culture is both a struggle for humanity and for a free humanity. In order to achieve real human freedom, we need to achieve economic, social, and political emancipation for the majority of the population of the world – but we also need to achieve cultural emancipation. We need to achieve a world where culture is free and where culture is enjoyed by all.

Definitions of culture based on elitist definitions are useless. In the end, culture is the social expression of all of the ideas of humanity – both good and bad. Elitist, usually reactionary, ideas about culture are useless. They usually deny the common basis of culture – that all of culture belongs to all of humanity.

Not all culture is necessarily 'good' – but all culture contributes to the development of humanity.

Culture will always be part of humanity. As long as humanity exists, culture will be part of humanity. Hopefully, the future struggle for a better society will allow culture to become truly free – in the hands of the majority.

I believe in a free humanity. I believe in a liberated humanity. I believe in an emancipated humanity. Freedom, liberation, and emancipation requires social struggle. I believe the struggle for a free culture is part of the struggle for a free humanity. I believe Socialism, as the struggle for the free development of humanity, is a vital part of the struggle for a free culture – for a free humanity.

The struggle for Socialism is the struggle for a free and emancipated humanity. The struggle for Socialism requires a social struggle for Socialism. This means culture, as part of society, is part of the social struggle for freedom.

Notes

1. R. Williams, Resources of Hope, (1989)
2. R. Williams, Culture is Ordinary, (1958)

(2013)

CHAPTER II

CULTURE AND HUMANITY

This essay is a study of culture and humanity — specifically a Socialist study of culture. All human societies produce culture. Culture is part of the reality of the development of human society. Culture is one of the great achievements of humanity. Indeed, culture is what has made humanity really human. If we wish to understand humans and humanity, we must understand culture and its social relationship with society. The social power of culture can be seen in both the politics of culture and the history of culture — the role of culture in politics and society. Culture can be explained by Historical Materialism. Cultural change can be explained by Historical Materialism. Historical Materialism suggests that human history develops due to material conditions, productive forces, social relations, social struggle, class struggle, human agency, and social revolution. History develops because of revolutionary social development — according to Historical Materialism. Culture develops because of revolutionary social development — according to Historical Materialism. All of humanity produces culture. All societies produce culture. Culture comes from society. Society produces culture. This means that we must understand the relationship between culture and humanity if we truly wish to understand humanity itself — and its revolutions of society and culture.

We can define culture. Culture is the social expression of social ideas. It is an expression of the popular creativity of humanity, as individuals, as classes, as societies, and as a species. Culture, in the end, is how any human society expresses its ideas and how any human society develops its ideas. Culture is the expression of human life. Culture is a social expression of human life. Culture is the practical expression of human life.1 This expression of culture means that culture is, necessarily, a social product of human society. Culture, according to Marx, is an expression of the social reality of a society, the social relations of a society, the social ideology of a society, and the social ideas of a society. Culture, for Marx, is part of 'the definite forms of social consciousness'. Culture is part of the ideological superstructure of human societies — the means of expressing ideas and social ideas.

There are many types of culture — art, music, literature, poetry, film, etc. All of these types of culture have emerged from the revolutionary development of culture and the revolutionary development of culture and society.

The development of culture is one of the most important developments of humanity. Humanity, as a species, would not have developed as well or as far without culture — without the revolutions of culture. Culture is part of the historical development of humanity.2

The development of culture has been a key part of the development of human freedom. Indeed, it has been a key part of the development of human struggles for social development and social freedom. Humanity, today, is the result of these types of social development. Social development, social struggle, and social revolution, today, has resulted in the possibility of a really free and human society – Socialism, a society based on the free development of each and the free development of all.3

Human history is the history of revolution. Indeed, the history of humanity is the history of social revolution: the Neolithic Revolution, the Urban Revolution, the Feudal Revolution, the Capitalist Revolution, and the contemporary struggle for Socialism. Human social history is also a product of revolution. Humanity, so far, has proceeded through various forms of society: Primitive Communism, Ancient society, Feudal society, Capitalist society, and the contemporary possibility of Socialism. This history of revolution includes culture. Human beings have revolutionised themselves and their societies through social, economic, political, intellectual, and cultural revolutions. Revolution, as defined by Marx, is the process of the revolutionary transformation of society. This revolutionary history has been part of humanity since the beginning of the human species. It has shaped both the development of humanity and the development of society and culture. Human history is the history of the revolutionary struggle for revolution – in order to achieve human freedom. The Socialist revolution, of today and the future, will hopefully produce a free humanity.

The development of culture has been part of humanity since the beginning of human evolution and since the beginning of the human species. Culture is part of the revolutionary development of humanity. Indeed, culture has been part of humanity since the development of humanity through its social struggles and social revolutions – the Neolithic Revolution, the Urban Revolution, the Feudal Revolution, the Capitalist Revolution, and the current struggle for Socialist Revolution. Human labour and human culture, through co-operation and social revolution, has been a key basis for human progress. Indeed, culture, as a process of labour, as a process of creation, can be considered part of the species-being of humanity — as defined by Marx.3

Culture is part of the process and progress of human liberation. Indeed, the development of culture is a vital part of the process of achieving human freedom. Humans, uniquely, create culture in order to achieve their self-realisation and their self-liberation. This is clear in terms of how Marx defined the process of human liberation as both a social, historical, and cultural process. As Marx wrote in 'The Economic and Philosophical Manuscripts of 1844' (1844): 'historical development is the process of human emancipation and rehabilitation'.4

Human history is the history of the development of society. It is the history of human struggle, class struggle, social struggle, and social revolution. Culture is an expression of this development. All of the social conflicts and social developments of human history — such as class conflict — have been vital to the development of society and culture.

Marxism, the theory and practice of working-class emancipation, has a powerful theory of the history and development of culture. For Marxism, culture is the social development of the ideas of human society. Culture, for Marxist theory, develops because of human activity, human struggle, and material development.

Marx's theory of Historical Materialism explains the development of culture. Historical Materialism shows that history develops because of material conditions, producing social relations and social revolutions. The material conditions of history produce certain 'modes of production', shaped around the economic base and the social superstructure of society, including culture, as shown by the base/superstructure model of historical development, and the agency of social revolution. History, for Marx, develops because of the development of the mode of production, the forces of production, and the relations of production, through production, development, class struggle, and social revolution.5 History is the product of material conditions, social struggle, class struggle, and social revolution. The socio-economic base of society produces the socio-ideological superstructure of society. Culture and changes in culture are part of the socio-ideological superstructure of society. Social change occurs, in the form of social revolution, due to conflict, specifically class conflict, within the mode of production and the relations of production. It is conflict, between these forms of production, which produces social development — in the form of class struggle and social revolution. The economic base of society produces a social superstructure — a social superstructure which includes culture. Culture, in the form of ideology, law, politics, religion, art and philosophy, is part of the social superstructure of human society. Historical development is the result of the development of both the base and superstructure of human societies — including culture. The development of culture is a historical development. Culture emerges as part of the social reality of humanity. The ultimate form of social development is social revolution. For Marx, culture is part of the social development of human society. For Marx, culture is part of what makes humanity, effectively, human — because it is a product of human activity. This means that culture is part of the dynamic of history, and the theory of Historical Materialism.

Culture emerges as part of the social reality of humanity due to the constant development of the mode of production, the forces of production, and the relations of production — in the form of class struggle, social production, and social revolution. In all of human history the development of culture occurs from the economic base of society and from the social base of society.

Social development is the basis for the development of culture. As a result, the history of social development is the basis for the history of culture. This point is consistent with the basic idea of Historical Materialism. It is material and social development which produces social and cultural change in human societies — because of the fact that social conditions determine consciousness, rather than consciousness determining social conditions. As Marx pointed out in 'Preface to a Contribution to the Critique of Political Economy' (1859): 'It is not the consciousness of men that determines their being, but, on the contrary, their social being that determines their consciousness'. Culture is an intellectual product, and a social product, of the social relationships in society. Culture is a product of the relationships between the mode of production, the forces of production, and the relations of production. Culture emerges, ultimately, out of social development and social relations.

Culture is an expression of human society and human development. Culture is an expression of the ideas of a society. It is the artistic expression of its ideas and ideals. All of the various forms of culture, from art to painting, from science to social organisation, can be connected to the social reality and the social progress of society — of humans and humanity. Culture, in the end, is a social product and a social relationship. Culture is connected to society. The history of society is the history of culture. The history of culture is the history of society.

Culture is an expression of economic society and economic development. The economic base of society produces the economic development which leads to social revolution, social progress, and cultural development. This economic determinism is the basis from which all forms of culture must emerge. Humanity can only produce culture when the correct social organisation and the correct social development exists to produce it. The power of culture, however, means that culture is itself a revolutionary force — but only within the boundaries of economic revolution and social revolution.

The beginning of society is the beginning of culture. Culture can only really start to emerge when humans co-operatively work to produce it — in the social organisation of society. All forms of society, from Primitive Communism to Feudalism, from Capitalism to Socialism, rely on the social organisation of society itself in order to produce their culture. The power of culture comes directly from its social organisation and its social connection. All of the great examples of art and culture, from all societies, would have been impossible to achieve without the social organisation of society. Every artist in history understands that their work is a product of their social environment. Every artist in history understands that their work is a product of their society. Historical Materialism can account for this social relationship — as the social relationship between an artist and their society is an example of the many forms of social relationship which make up human societies.

All societies produce culture. This is obvious if we look at any human society, at any point in the development of human society. Every society which has emerged as part of humanity has produced culture and forms of culture. Culture has been part of humanity since the beginning of humanity and human societies — since the origins of humanity out of the process of biological evolution and social evolution. Every society which has emerged from human history has produced culture and forms of culture.6 Every society has produced a useful culture — a culture which helps to progress that society and to maintain that society. All human culture is the product of all human society. Studies of culture always need to recognise the revolutionary dynamic and revolutionary nature of culture. Culture is a revolutionary reality of humanity. Culture is a universal reality of humanity. Every society takes part in the production of culture. Every individual can take part in the production of culture. The social power of culture shows that culture has a social basis and social relationship. Every Socialist and every Marxist knows the social power of culture. All studies of culture can see its importance — both to society and to social revolution.

The basic relationship between humanity and culture is a social relationship. One produces the other. They produce each other. In the end culture cannot exist without society and society cannot exist without culture. This fact shows that the development of culture and society are linked. This fact also shows that the development of culture and society are necessarily social developments, economic developments, political developments, and historical developments. In order to understand culture and humanity we must understand the various connections which outline the connection between culture and society. This connection is crucial to understand for three reasons. The first is the need to understand the connection between culture and society. The second reason is the need to understand the connection between culture and Capitalism. The third reason is the need to understand the connection between culture and Socialism. In order to achieve Socialism, a society based on equality and co-operation, we must understand the basic connection between culture and society.

The historical development of culture can be explained by Historical Materialism. Culture develops through the process of the class struggle and the process of the contradictions of the mode of production and the relations of production. Marx outlined this, quite simply, in his 'Preface to a Contribution of the Critique of Political Economy' (1859). His point was that culture cannot exist outside of social development and human development. Every advance in culture was preceded by other types of social conflict and social revolution. The plays of Shakespeare came from the social struggle of the Wars of the Roses and the Tudor period. The novels of Dickens came from the realities of the Industrial Revolution. The artistic revolution of the Renaissance came from the social revolutions and economic revolutions of the Renaissance, in the 15th century, and from the crisis of the 14th century. Every cultural revolution can be linked to a greater social revolution. The materialist roots of culture are shown by any basic analysis of culture, by the materialist conception of history.7

The history of culture shows the connection between culture and society. No culture has emerged artificially from society — instead, history shows that culture only emerges from the historical development of society. The connection between culture and society is a concrete reality and a concrete force in human history.

Culture changes in two ways — through slow social reform or through social revolution. The history of culture is the history of societies producing changes in culture through such reform or such revolution. It is these two types of social and cultural change that have produced the greatest social revolutions of human history. The main forms of social revolution in human history have been the Neolithic Revolution, the Urban Revolution, the Feudal Revolution, the Capitalist Revolution, and the current struggle for Socialist Revolution.

Revolutionary struggles for change in culture have dominated the history of culture. The Renaissance, the Scientific Revolution, the invention of painting, the invention of writing, the invention of art, were all produced by social revolutions which became cultural revolutions.8

Change in human culture has usually come from revolution. Revolution is the process of the revolutionary transformation of society. It is a social or political process which results in social transformation. The two main forms of revolution, social revolution and political revolution, result in serious social change. All of the great revolutions of human history have produced cultural revolutions. All of the great social revolutions of human history have produced cultural revolutions. The neolithic revolution, the urban revolution, the rise of Ancient society, the rise of Feudal society, the rise of Capitalist society, and the possible rise of Socialist society, were major social revolutions in human history. All of these revolutions produced economic revolutions which created cultural revolutions. The English Revolution of 1640, the American Revolution of 1776, the French Revolution of 1789, the Russian Revolution of 1917, the Chinese Revolution of 1949, the Cuban Revolution of 1959, the Iranian Revolution of 1979, and the revolutions of today, all created political revolutions which created cultural revolutions. The revolutions of culture, from the neolithic revolution to modern society, from the Renaissance to the internet age, have been shaped by the economic revolutions and social revolutions which produced these cultural revolutions. The power of social revolution, in the history of culture and society, is impossible to ignore. The power of social revolution is the revolutionary force which drives forward both culture and society. It is social revolution, in the end, which produces the greatest forms of cultural revolution, and cultural change. Indeed, social revolution produces the most innovative and revolutionary forms of new culture.

The politics of culture shows the revolutionary connection between culture and society. The politics of culture also show the connection between culture and revolution. Human culture has changed, throughout history, because of social change and social development — but it has also changed due to the reality of political revolution, social revolution, and economic revolution. Major changes in the history of culture have usually occurred because of a wider social revolution imposing social change — or achieving the basis for a successful cultural revolution. All revolutionary struggles produce their own form of culture and revolution — even if simply in terms of the revolutionary theory and the revolutionary ideas they use in order to achieve social revolution and political revolution. The political development of societies, throughout history and politics, through revolution and counter-revolution, have shaped the basis by which culture has developed and the basis by which culture has changed. The historical development of humanity, since the neolithic revolution, is the basis by which almost all culture has been created, shaped, and changed. The historical development of society, through changing modes of production, has produced the basis by which the revolutions of culture have taken place. Revolution and social change are some of the key means by which cultures change and adapt. It is impossible to write the history of culture, or the history of the social development of culture, without understanding the history of revolution and counter-revolution. Revolutions of culture seek to develop culture. Counter-Revolutions of culture seek to maintain culture as it is. All social revolutions produce cultural revolutions. All economic revolutions produce cultural revolutions. The French Revolution of 1789 produced a cultural revolution. The transition from Feudalism to Capitalism (1450-1850) produced a cultural revolution. The Russian Revolution of 1917 produced a cultural revolution. The possible revolution to achieve Socialism will probably produce a cultural revolution. In the world today, the link between culture and revolution is very clear. We can see the link in all the revolutions of the past and all the revolutions of the future. It is likely that the revolutions of the future will produce cultural change and cultural revolution. This assumption simply follows the basic assumptions of Historical Materialism. A revolution in society produces a revolution in culture.9

Human history has led up to today. Today we live in a Capitalist society and in a Capitalist culture. This society, and this culture, has been created and shaped by the historical developments of human history. Capitalist society and Capitalist culture are the dominant forms of society and culture in the world today. We must understand this if a better form of society and culture is to emerge today — in order to create Socialism and a Socialist culture. This means that we need to understand Capitalist society and Capitalist culture. This means we need to create Socialism. This means we need to create a Socialist culture.10

If we are to understand the connection between culture and society, we must understand the connection between culture and society today. Culture, and society, today, is being shaped by the economic society which exists today. That economic society is the society of Capitalism.

Capitalism shapes culture. This has been an obvious fact since the rise of Capitalism and the fall of Feudalism. The rise of Capitalist culture, from the 19th century, has come to dominate the bulk of culture which exists in human society today. The strength of this culture has gone from strength to strength —especially since the victory of Capitalism in the Cold War. Despite this it is now clear that the culture of Capitalism is beginning to run into serious problems and serious issues — due to the crisis of Capitalism and the crisis of the Capitalist system. We cannot yet know what will happen to Capitalism or Capitalist culture in the coming decades, but it is obvious to most that Capitalism is once again in crisis. Capitalism is in crisis. Capitalist culture is also in crisis.

Culture shapes Capitalism. Culture has been one of the best tools for Capitalism since the emergence of Capitalism. Indeed, culture has been used by Capitalism at every level of the Capitalist system — from advertising to propaganda, from politics to ideology. Every form of Capitalism, since the end of Feudalism, has used culture in some form or another – in order to justify and maintain Capitalism. Culture is a key tool for any Capitalist society. This means that the development of culture helps to shape the development of Capitalism – in Capitalist societies. Yet the ability of culture to promote Capitalism is also beginning to decline today — as the structure of Capitalism itself weakens due to the reality of the crisis of Capitalism. In this process the opportunity emerges for new and different types of culture to emerge. Capitalism will not be overthrown by criticising its culture — but it will be weakened by the decline of its culture and by the decline of Capitalism itself.11 Capitalism, today, can no longer rely on culture to help maintain Capitalism.

The development of Capitalism shapes culture. Capitalism has existed since the transition from Feudalism to Capitalism — the transition between 1450 and 1850. The development of Capitalism has led to the development of both culture itself and the development of a Capitalist culture. The development of Capitalist culture has always sought to uphold the economic development and the intellectual development of Capitalism. Capitalist art, and Capitalist culture, tends to reinforce the economic goals and the political goals of Capitalism. This has made culture a vital part of modern Capitalism and modern Capitalist society. Capitalism is, today, the dominant form of society and culture in the world.

The economic development of Capitalism shapes culture. Capitalism, in the last two hundred years, has created major economic forces. These economic forces have spread across the world and have shaped the world — both for the better and for the worse. Economic development always leads to a development of culture — even if just in terms of the social development of the means of production. Capitalism, for the first time in history, has created a truly global culture and a truly universal culture. Capitalism has also created the forces and the social forces which can create Socialism and a better culture. Capitalism has produced the working class — a class which is capable of making Socialism. The economic development of Capitalism has been a major triumph for Capitalism — but it has also produced the social forces and the economic forces which will lead to the downfall of Capitalism. Capitalism will be replaced by Socialism. Capitalist culture will be replaced by Socialist culture.

The political development of Capitalism shapes culture. The political development of Capitalism, in the last two hundred years, has been shaped by the development of culture. Capitalism has developed many different types of political movements and political ideas — Liberalism, Conservatism, Neo-Liberalism, Neo-Conservatism, Fascism, and Nazism. This has led to both revolutions and counter-revolutions for culture. The French Revolution brought about a revolution for culture. The triumph of Nazism brought about a counter-revolution for culture. The history of Capitalism is the history of both revolution and counter-revolution for culture. The political development of Capitalism shows that Capitalism is capable of both progressing the development of culture and capable of crushing the development of culture. Capitalism is capable of both culture and Barbarism. This fact is shown by the historical development of Capitalism —since its origins out of Feudalism. Future developments for culture and for art will have to be based on a different type of society —one which overcomes the limits of Capitalist society and Capitalist culture. Humanity needs to think about the struggle for Socialism. Humanity needs Socialism.

The relationship between culture and society, today, is shaped by Capitalism. The politics of culture shows the connection between culture and society. All class societies produce culture — but they produce culture in line with the ideas of their ruling class, and the interests of their ruling class. Indeed, the majority of the ideas in any culture are usually the ideas of the ruling class. In Feudal society, culture was dominated by the interests of the Feudal Lords. In Capitalist society, culture is dominated by the interests of the capitalist class. The majority of culture produced by class society tends to be in line with the interests of the ruling class. This is because for most of human history the ruling class, of most societies, tends to dominate the cultural politics of society. Our culture, today, is a Capitalist culture because the capitalist class, the ruling class of Capitalist society, dominates the culture of our society. Only very rarely in the history of class societies does this tendency towards the ruling class dominating culture break down — in revolutionary periods and revolutionary struggles. The free development of culture, in class societies, is impossible. The only way to achieve the free development of culture is to abolish class society. This is why Socialism, the struggle to achieve a liberated society, is the social revolution which can produce a real human culture. Socialism will revolutionise culture.12

Socialism can liberate culture and society. If we wish to see a really free culture, we need to abolish Class society. So long as Class society exists the interests of Class society will dictate the type of culture which is produced and the direction of the development of culture. A free culture requires a free society. A free society requires a classless society. In Capitalist society the capitalist class dominates culture and shapes culture. In Socialist society the working class dominates culture and shapes culture. In Socialist society, Humanity itself dominates culture and shapes culture.

Socialist culture is a culture which is based on Socialism. Socialism is a society in which co-operation and equality are the basis of society. Socialism is also a society which is based on the free development of each and the free development of all. This means that Socialism is a powerful force for the development of human culture — and the development of a liberated culture. The power of a Socialist society would lead to a culture in which all people are free to pursue their interests and their culture. Marx understood the revolutionary power of culture to liberate humanity. His vision of Socialism was based not only on economic liberation, political liberation, and social liberation but also on cultural liberation. He believed in a vision of a Socialist society where the 'free development of each is the condition for the free development of all'. This vision of Socialism is the vision of a Socialist culture.

We live in a Capitalist society. The basic culture of contemporary culture and popular culture is shaped by Capitalism. This has been the reality of the development of culture and society since the triumph of Capitalism and the triumph of the Industrial Revolution. In order to achieve a free culture, we must establish Socialism.13

We can sum up culture. Culture is the ideas of human society. Culture is an expression of the ideas, principles, and values of human society. It is the social production of ideas in human societies. It is the social expression of social ideas. Society produces culture. Culture helps to shape society. The development of culture depends on social development and historical development. Culture has progressed through various historical stages — Primitive Communism, Ancient Society, Feudalism, Capitalism, and on to Socialism. Culture is part of what makes humanity into humanity. Culture is part of what makes humans into humans. This type of social development is crucial towards achieving the social liberation of humanity.

We can also sum up how society produces culture. Culture is produced by the social relations of society. Changes in culture occur when there is conflict in the social relations of production and conflict between the social relations of production, the forces of production, and the mode of production. If the social conflicts of society become revolutionary this sparks a social revolution — which changes the mode of production, the forces of production and the social relations of production. This type of social revolution brings about changes in culture. This type of social revolution brings about cultural revolution.

Historical Materialism can explain culture. Historical Materialism can explain the revolutions in culture. Culture cannot be explained by simply referring to the innate superiority of one culture over another — as Capitalists and Fascists do. Culture can only be explained by the material developments of humanity — the material development of the liberation of humanity. Culture can only be explained by its social development and its social connection. What makes a bad culture, or a good culture, is generally its attitude about humanity. A bad culture is that culture which holds back social development and social freedom. A good culture is that culture which helps to develop social freedom. The best type of culture would be that culture which helps to bring about complete social freedom and the abolition of classes — Socialism and Communism.

Humanity deserves a truly human culture. Humanity deserves a humanist culture. This type of culture, one which is free and universal, can only come from a society which is based on co-operation and equality. Socialism, by developing co-operation and abolishing classes, produces the basis for that type of human culture. Socialist Humanism, in particular, focuses on the idea that human liberation can only come from human self-liberation. Human culture, to be a truly free human culture, must be liberated from the realities of Class, exploitation, and oppression. Only when this has been achieved will we have a culture which is truly human. Capitalist culture must be replaced by Socialist culture.

The social power of art and culture is obvious. The social power of art and culture can often shape society. The social power of art and culture can often improve society. If we wish to see a truly free art and culture, then the only way to achieve this is to break with Capitalism and to establish Socialism. The reason for this is that Capitalism, as a system based on exploitation and hierarchy, is not interested in the development of art or culture. Socialism, on the other hand, is interested in the development of art and culture, because Socialism seeks to eliminate exploitation and hierarchy — and unleash the creative development of art and culture. In place of a culture which is dominated by the interest of Capitalism we need a culture which is dominated by the interests of humanity.14

The liberation of culture will only come via Socialism. Socialism is the only type of society which has the economic development to create culture while also having the social power to liberate culture. In the end the social development and social revolution of humanity will lead to Socialism — as a process of the historical development of society. This will lead to not only a better society but also to a better culture. The social power of this new form of culture will be to liberate humanity. It will allow humanity to be able to both produce culture and to enjoy culture. Culture will become the common inheritance of humanity.

The role of the artist is vital in understanding the relationship between culture and society. The artist helps to produce culture. The artist helps to shape culture. The artist helps to advance culture.

Culture is produced by people, artists, by individuals, by collectives, and by wider society. It is produced by ordinary people. This is a collective process. When we think of culture we often think of the artist or the individual artist — developing their work in isolation from society. We often think of such artists working alone, as individuals in isolation, producing revolutions in culture purely through their individual genius. This is not how revolutions in art or culture have usually happened — either in history or today. This is not how artists or individual artists work either. Culture and the real development of culture is inherently a collective process and a collective progress. Individual artists can achieve major developments in culture, as individuals, but every major revolution in culture, in history, has occurred because of collective developments – by many artists and through society. No artist can escape from the reality that their work and their art is part of a wider social process and a wider social progress. Every producer of culture exists in a wider social relationship and a wider social reality — from which emerges both culture and ideas. Indeed, the best forms of artistic revolution, in history and in the present, occurred because of human co-operation. The Renaissance, for example, was a social revolution – it relied on human co-operation. The Renaissance (1450-1600) was based on centuries of social revolution and cultural revolution — revolutions which developed because of countless workers, artists, artisans, thinkers, and craftsmen. The Renaissance was a social revolution in 15th century Italy before it became an artistic revolution. The Renaissance was based on social revolution and not simply individual genius. Achieving revolutions in art and culture usually depends on a wider society or a wider social struggle. Individual genius does exist in culture and in the arts, from Shakespeare to Brecht, but all artists, at some point or another, live in society or engage with society. Their art is a product of society and a product of their engagement with society. No artist, no individual, can divorce themselves from society without losing some part of what makes them human. Even the most individualistic writer, artist, film director, or poet, cannot escape this wider connection with society. Their work influences society and culture — but their work is ultimately determined by society and culture. Artists do make revolution – but only through social revolution.15

Percy Shelley, the great British radical poet of the 19th century, understood the connection between the individual artist and wider society. He understood that humanity, in the end, is connected. No artist can escape their social reality, just as no culture can escape its wider social reality. Shelley understood the reality of the social connection between culture and society. Shelley understood that all culture ultimately is connected to the society which produced it. Shelley understood that all artists are connected to society. Society is shaped by its culture — but culture is determined by society. No artist is an isolated individual in the end. Every artist is a product of society. Shelley outlined the mutual connection of humanity in his epic poem 'Prometheus Unbound':

> MAN, one harmonious soul of many a soul,
> Whose nature is its own divine control,
> Where all things flow to all, as rivers to the sea;
> Familiar acts are beautiful through love;
> Labour, and pain, and grief, in life's green grove
> Sport like tame beasts, none knew how gentle they could be.16

Karl Marx, the great Socialist and Communist, understood that human development and human liberation, in the form of human culture, relies on human beings and human co-operation. For Marx, the ultimate development of human history is the struggle for human liberation — through the development of the mode of production, the forces of production, the relations of production, and the reality of class conflict, class struggle, and social revolution. Marx, in the end, always understood that all human culture is a co-operative process — a process which must lead to freedom for all, through Socialism and Communism. Human beings can only fully realise themselves, and their own liberation, through co-operation. For Marx, humans are humans because they are able to labour as universal and free beings. This outline of humans, and humanity, is vital to Marx's theory of humanism — of human liberation. For Marx, humans are a natural species, a species which is part of nature and also a species which can change nature. He fully expressed this in 'Economic and Philosophical Manuscripts of 1844' (1844):

> Man is directly a natural being. As a natural being and as a living natural being, he is on the one hand endowed with natural powers, vital powers — he is an active natural being. These forces exist in him as tendencies and abilities — as instincts. On the other hand, as a natural, corporeal, sensuous objective being he is a suffering, conditioned and limited creature, like animals and plants. That is to say, the objects of his instincts exist outside him, as objects independent of him; yet these objects are objects that he needs — essential objects, indispensable to the manifestation and confirmation of his essential powers.17

Marx outlined a fully humanist theory of human beings. He argued that humans are human because of their ability to labour and their ability to express their humanity as universal. For Marx, the real basis of humanity, our species-being, is our ability to labour, and our ability to have agency as human beings. He fully expressed this in 'Economic and Philosophical Manuscripts of 1844' (1844):

> Man is a species-being, not only because in practice and in theory he adopts the species (his own as well as those of other things) as his object, but — and this is only another way of expressing it — also because he treats himself as the actual, living species; because he treats himself as a universal and therefore a free being.18

Marx outlined the real social basis of human development — in the development of production, the development of labour, and the development of social relations. Co-operation is the basis of the advancement of any human society or any human society. Marx outlined this in his pamphlet, 'Wage Labour and Capital' (1847):

> In the process of production, human beings work not only upon nature, but also upon one another. They produce only by working together in a specified manner and reciprocally exchanging their activities. In order to produce, they enter into definite connections and relations to one another, and only within these social connections and relations does their influence upon nature operate — i.e., does production take place. … These social relations between the producers, and the conditions under which they exchange their activities and share in the total act of production, will naturally vary according to the character of the means of production.19

Marx outlined the role of culture and cultural development in the development of humanity. Marx's theory of historical materialism, his theory of history, understood that history develops because of the development of material conditions, the mode of production, the forces of production, the means of production, the relations of production, class conflict, class struggle, and social revolution. History develops because of the conflicts of the material base and superstructure of society — which leads to class conflict, class struggle, and social revolution. Culture, as part of the superstructure of society, plays a role in history and development. For Marx, culture and cultural development plays a role in the development of human history and human society. Marx, in his theory of Historical Materialism, shows the importance of culture and ideology to overall historical development. Marx outlined this in 'Preface to a Contribution to the Critique of Political Economy' (1859):

> In the social production of their existence, men inevitably enter into definite relations, which are independent of their will, namely relations of production appropriate to a given stage in the development of their material forces of production. The totality of these relations of production constitutes the economic structure of society, the real foundation, on which arises a legal and political superstructure and to which correspond definite forms of social consciousness. The mode of production of material life conditions the general process of social, political, and intellectual life. It is not the consciousness of men that determines their existence, but their social existence that determines their consciousness. At a certain stage of development, the material productive forces of society come into conflict with the existing relations of production or — this merely expresses the same thing in legal terms — with the property relations within the framework of which they have operated hitherto. From forms of development of the productive forces these relations turn into their fetters. Then begins an era of social revolution. The changes in the economic foundation lead sooner or later to the transformation of the whole immense superstructure.20

The basis of any real advance in human society, for Marx, is the struggle of achieving real human liberation and real human freedom. This can only be achieved by achieving a society which overcomes the economic basis and the social basis of exploitation and oppression. For Marx, the only way to achieve a liberated society is to achieve a society which abolishes class and class antagonisms — a society based on the free development of each as the condition for the free development of all. Human culture, if it is to be a liberated culture, must be a real human culture — a culture of Socialism.

Marx outlined his ideas about the necessity of human liberation as the basis for human culture in his long outline of the humanism of Communism — a society based on the free development of each and the free development of all. The ultimate development of culture and society can only occur in the form of the advanced development of humanity itself, via the positive development of a stateless, classless, democratic, society — a society of Socialism, a society of Communism. Marx outlined this idea in 'Economic and Philosophical Manuscripts of 1844' (1844):

> Communism, as fully developed naturalism, equals humanism, and as fully developed humanism equals naturalism; it is the genuine resolution of the conflict between man and nature, and between man and man, the true resolution of the conflict between existence and being, between objectification and self-affirmation, between freedom and necessity, between individual and species. It is the solution of the riddle of history and knows itself to be the solution.21

The connection between culture and society is a social relationship. The connection between culture and society is a political relationship. In the struggle for a better world the struggle for a better culture and a better society are vital. When we look at culture today, we can see the problems of Capitalist culture. When we look at the problems of Capitalism, we often find solutions to those problems — in the form of Socialism. The ideas of Marx, Engels, Lenin, and Trotsky, can still help in developing the solutions which we need — in order to face Capitalism and to achieve Socialism. From this we might be able to achieve a better culture and a better society. We might even achieve human freedom.

Culture is a social expression of the ideas of humanity. Indeed, culture is the social expression of humanity. Culture, because it is produced by all of humanity, belongs to all of humanity. Ordinary people produce culture through their day-to-day lives and through their day-to-day struggles. It is through the process of production and struggle that culture is generated. This means that culture, in the end, is the intellectual expression of ordinary people, in the construction of their own lives. This means that all people have a right to culture and a right to produce culture. All people have a right to the ideas and social power of culture. Ordinary working-class people are the real social basis for human culture – because ordinary working-class people, today, are the overwhelming majority of the human species. The only way to build a truly effective and humane culture is to build a culture in which the overwhelming majority of humanity takes part in producing it. This means that the only way to have a free culture is to have Socialism. Only Socialism, a society based on the free development of each and the free development of all, can produce culture for each and culture for all.

All culture, in the world today, is shaped by Capitalism and by Capitalist culture. It is impossible, today, for any culture, under Capitalism, to be purely free of Capitalism. If we wish to have a genuine and free culture, a culture free from Capitalism, then we must abolish Capitalism — and establish Socialism.

The connection between culture and revolution is a social relationship. We can see, throughout history, that the progress of culture is linked, directly, to the progress of social revolution. The social progress of culture can be measured by the progress of social revolution. Social revolution, in the end, shows the connection between culture and humanity.

Notes

1. R. Williams, Culture and Society, (1958)
2. R. Williams, The Long Revolution, (1961)
3. K. Marx, Economic and Philosophical Manuscripts of 1844, (1844)
4. K. Marx, Economic and Philosophical Manuscripts of 1844, (1844)
5. K. Marx and F. Engels, The Communist Manifesto, (1848)
6. V. G. Childe, Man Makes Himself, (1936)
7. C. Caudwell, Illusion and Reality, (1937)
8. C. Caudwell, Illusion and Reality, (1937)
9. R. Williams, Culture and Society, (1958)
10. E.P. Thompson, Socialist Humanism, (1957)
11. C. Caudwell, Illusion and Reality, (1937)
12. C. Caudwell, Studies in a Dying Culture, (1938)
13. K. Marx, Economic and Philosophical Manuscripts of 1844, (1844)
14. K. Marx, Economic and Philosophical Manuscripts of 1844, (1844)
15. K. Marx, Economic and Philosophical Manuscripts of 1844, (1844)
16. P. Shelley, Prometheus Unbound, (1820)
17. K. Marx, Economic and Philosophical Manuscripts of 1844, (1844)
18. K. Marx, Economic and Philosophical Manuscripts of 1844, (1844)
19. K. Marx, Wage Labour and Capital, (1847)
20. K. Marx, Preface to a Contribution to the Critique of Political Economy (1859)
21. K. Marx and F. Engels, The Communist Manifesto, (1848)

(2016)

CHAPTER III

CULTURE AND THE FUTURE

This short essay is a study of culture and the future. It is a Socialist study of culture and how culture might develop in the future. Culture is the social expression of human ideas. Culture will continue to develop for as long as society continues to exist. Hopefully, society, today, will develop towards Socialism — and towards a Socialist culture.

The history of culture shows that culture emerges from society. The politics of culture shows that culture emerges from society. This means that the development of culture is both social and political. The argument of this essay, from a Socialist standpoint, is that culture is ultimately a product of society. Where society goes, so too does culture. Where culture goes, so too does society. The future of culture depends, in the end, on the development of society – through social struggle and social revolution. Culture can be individual and individualistic — the product of individual views and individual emotions — but culture is ultimately connected to the society which produced the society and the culture. The dynamic of society and culture, in the end, is that society will always determine culture. Even the most individual example of culture is still a product of a society. It is likely that the relationship between culture and society, between culture and social relationships, will continue. Society will continue to produce culture. Society will continue to be connected to culture. Of course, this assumption rests on the broader assumption that humanity will continue to develop — both now and in the future. Humanity might not survive the coming centuries — due to the possibility of nuclear war or environmental collapse — but if humanity does survive into the future, it is likely that some form of culture will continue to be part of the development of society and the development of individuals. Hopefully, that culture will be under a better form of society — a free society, an equal society, a more human society, a more developed society, a more Socialist society. Society will continue to produce culture and culture will continue to produce culture itself — but the hope must always be for a better humanity, and a better culture, in the future. Currently the majority of culture, in the world today, is produced by

Capitalism and by Capitalist society. It is likely, in the future, that culture will either continue to be produced by Capitalist society — with all its misery, oppression, and exploitation — or humanity will progress, forward, towards Socialism and towards Communism. The choice for society and for culture, today, is a simple one — the choice between Capitalism and Socialism, the choice between Barbarism and Socialism.1 Hopefully society and culture will advance – towards Socialism, towards a society based on the free development of each and the free development of all.

The future of culture is connected to the future of society. Culture is changed by revolution. The future is always a revolutionary future — given the social reality that the future will always be different than the past, given the nature of revolution and social change. Culture has always been interested in the future. Indeed, the best culture has always engaged with the future and the idea of the future. The future has always been a key topic for culture — either in terms of thinking about the possibilities of the future or the threats of the future. The development of modern society, after the Industrial Revolution, generated a need to think about the future in real terms – both for society and for culture. The Industrial Revolution showed that the world could be changed – and that society itself could be changed. Indeed, the Industrial Revolution created the basis for a revolution in society and in culture. The French Revolution of 1789 generated some of the best writers and best culture of all times — as did the Russian Revolution of 1917. All of the great social revolutions of history, in the end, create the conditions for new and revolutionary culture. Human culture, in the end, changes because of social revolution. New culture, in history and in society, often expresses the possibilities of revolution — and the possibilities of the future. Every serious left-wing writer, today, in one way or another, is engaged in the process of using culture to both explain society and to change society — in a process which engages with both the present and the future. Culture, at its most revolutionary, is often about engaging with the future — and the possibility of a revolutionary future. Either we will seize the future, and achieve a Socialist future, or we shall suffer the reality of Barbarism.2

If culture is to progress, today, it is vital for culture to think about both the present and the future. Culture, if it is to develop, cannot limit itself to simply the great ideas and ideals of the past. The history of great ideas and artistic work is important but revolutionary developments cannot be achieved by simply repeating the past — this is true in all areas of ideas and culture. Culture, today, really needs to engage with society today and the possible future of society. The best examples of culture always do this, but it is vital today — simply in terms of developing new ideas, both in culture and in society. There is also the need for culture to engage with society today in order to develop ideas for the future — both for culture and for society. The future is not static. The future can be changed. The future can be changed by social revolution. This means that artists have both a role and place in developing the ideas and structures of the future. This means that writers and artists have an obligation to engage with society, to write about society, and to help change society for the better. Culture can be either a revolutionary force for the future or a counter-revolutionary force for the future. If culture wants to have a good future, to develop and progress, as part of a good society, then it will need to be revolutionary. Culture will need to engage with the political developments and social developments of today — and take part in the revolutions of today. Culture is a vital part of both the intellectual revolution of today and the social revolution of today. Indeed, in intellectual terms, culture could become a revolutionary force — for intellectual revolution. In intellectual terms culture has a role to play in both the criticism of Capitalist society and the building of a Socialist society. Culture needs to become part of the revolutionary force in society today — in the struggle for Socialism.3

Culture, today, needs to think about the future. Culture needs to write about the future. Culture needs to help us create the future. Culture needs to engage with the reality of today and the reality of the future. Indeed, it can be argued that culture always needs to think about the future in order to develop as part of human culture. Culture has always been at its best when it is thinking about both today and the future — about society today and society in the future. This has always been a true statement for Left artists and Left writers — who understand that social change is inevitable, and that social change needs to be fought for. Culture needs to be revolutionary, today, because the world is always being changed by revolution — either to maintain Capitalism or to create Socialism. The best artists understand that their ideas are being shaped by a society which is being constantly changed by revolution. The world today is being shaped by revolution — by economic revolution, social revolution, political revolution, cultural revolution, intellectual revolution, and scientific revolution. All of human society is being changed by revolution. This reality of revolution is a reality for all human society. This has certainly been the case since the creation of the modern world — with the development of modern society, modern industry, and modern revolution. The sheer pace of social change, social development, and social revolution, since 1789, has forced most writers and artists to think hard about the connection between themselves, their work, their culture, and their society. Indeed, revolutionary times have always called for revolutionary culture. Indeed, future times have always called for future culture. The future is revolutionary — simply due to the sheer pace of social change and historical change generated by the last two centuries and by the current century. Writers, as literary people, always need to think about the future simply because shaping the future is a key part of modern society and modern development. The future is rapidly developing today – because of the nature of social development today. The pace of social change also demands that society think about its future — about what direction society is heading. This means that society is always looking for new and revolutionary ideas. The ideas of culture, if they are to remain useful, powerful, and relevant, need to engage with this reality — a reality being created today and tomorrow. In social and cultural terms this means society must engage with both the world around them and the world which might emerge in the future.4

Culture tells us a great deal about how any society sees itself — and sees its future. If we want to understand how a society thinks about itself and its future, we need to understand its culture. In our society the struggle of culture is the struggle between Capitalism and Socialism. This struggle is present in all culture today — between Capitalism and Socialism.5

The politics of culture means that culture cannot be disconnected from society. This political connection means that the future of culture will always be connected to society — to human society.6

The future of culture is an important social question today. The future of culture will probably be determined by the history of culture and by the history of society. Culture, in the end, will be transformed by the revolutions which are shaping, and re-shaping, society.7

Culture tells us a great deal about how any individual sees themselves — and sees the future. In many ways many of the best examples of cultural ideas have been about the relationship between individuals and their vision of the future. Writers who write about the future might be wrong about the future — about future developments and future society — but their work also gives an insight into their understanding of themselves, their hopes, their fears, and their dreams — for the future and for the future of society. This is often more useful for humanity than ideas which simply speak of present times or of past times. The British Communist poets of the 1930s — who dreamed of Socialist Revolution and Socialist society — might have been wrong about the exact nature of the future, given the ongoing struggle between revolution and counter-revolution today, but their work reflects both their ideas and their times. The struggle for the future, for a Socialist society, still continues. In many ways such works about the future help to explain the ideas of the individual artist and their connection to society. In many ways the Socialist writer is the best sort of writer to write about the future.

Changes in culture always produce changes in artists and writers. This means that every artist needs to always engage both with their society, their times, and the future. No artist can escape from the social reality which informs culture and society. Indeed, even the most individualistic artist cannot detach themselves purely from society — especially if they want their work to engage with society. William Blake, for example, a radical 19th century British poet, who produced some of the greatest pieces of art in British history, still engaged with society at large and with social developments at large. Blake, in many ways, is one of the best examples of a poet who, even at his most radical, still engaged with the social realities and social revolutions of his times — indeed, his poems became part of the wider social revolutions of the 19th century. He was also an artist who was committed to social change and to social revolution. Blake is a great example of a radical artist – one who was committed to social revolution. Blake shows that even the most individual artist is always connected to wider society. Blake shows how an artist can be a revolutionary artist.

It is impossible to completely predict the future of culture. This is because culture still requires some imagination to produce — which is often difficult to predict and often impossible to predict. Culture might develop in various ways in the future — by becoming more engaged with society or less engaged with society. What can be predicted, however, is that culture will continue to be part of modern society and part of the intellectual development of modern society. Indeed, from the perspective of politics and intellectual history, this makes culture very useful for understanding the development of a society as it moves forward into the future. Radical culture can help to make sense of a society, its revolutions, and its changes. Indeed, radical culture can sometimes point towards the possibility of real social change – the possibility of human freedom.

Culture might change in the future, but it will always be a product of human society. Culture will remain part of human society — because it is made by human beings who are part of human society. This is a simple reality of both culture and society — as culture will never be able to completely divorce itself from society so long as human beings produce culture. This is a social relationship — because culture is a product of its social environment and its intellectual environment.

Culture will always develop and react to the reality of society and the reality of changing times. Culture always has to engage with society, with revolution, and with counter-revolution, in order to remain important and to remain socially relevant. This aspect of culture will always be part of culture – both now and in the future.

If we really want to think about the future of culture, we need to engage with the reality of society today. We need to engage with the reality of where art comes from and how it is shaped by the revolutions of society. Social development, in the end, is the basis for all art. Culture, as part of art, is part of social development — and it is social development which will determine the future of culture.

Society, today, is faced with the choice of either revolution or counter-revolution. Society, today, cannot ignore this social reality. Society cannot ignore that the very nature of society is being changed and shaped by revolution. Society has a simple choice — either engage with the reality of the revolutions of society or become an irrelevant society. Culture is faced with a key choice today — either Socialism or Capitalism.

In order for culture to develop, today, and in the future, culture needs to engage with the reality of politics and society today — particularly in the struggle between Capitalism and Socialism. Culture today needs to engage with Socialism and with the ideas of Socialism. Culture, today and in the future, needs to engage with Socialism.

Capitalism dominates the world and most of society today.8 This means that most culture, today, is shaped by Capitalism. It is likely that for as long as Capitalism exists its hegemony will continue to dominate most forms of culture.

Culture is being shaped by Capitalist society — in various ways. If we truly wish to understand the reality of culture today, we must understand the reality of culture and society under Capitalism.9 It is only then that we can perhaps begin to think about alternatives for the future of culture — for Socialism, for Socialist society, and for Socialist culture.

Culture will change in the future. It will change because Capitalist society is generating crisis and social revolution, hopefully resulting in Socialism. Capitalism has unleashed social forces which it can no longer control. This means that Capitalism will always be challenged by the possibility of Socialism — until the day in which Capitalism is finally replaced by Socialism.10

Culture which supports Capitalism sees the future in Capitalist terms. Culture which opposes Capitalism sees the future in Socialist terms. This division creates a great deal of the conflict in culture — between the Right and the Left. The social struggle of today, between Capitalism and Socialism, is reflected in the intellectual struggle between the Right and the Left — which includes literature and culture. If we want to understand the intellectual conflicts in culture today, between old and new, between Right and Left, the majority of that conflict can be explained by the wider political struggles surrounding societies and their culture. Indeed, it is impossible for a serious writer, today, to ignore the social struggle between Capitalism and Socialism. The work of every writer and every artist can be connected to the social struggle of today — between Capitalism and Socialism. This social struggle is evident in all parts of the world. The struggle within culture, today, is the struggle between the Right and the Left of culture — between Capitalism and Socialism. Some of the best writers and artists, today, understand this political implication of their work and this social implication of their work. No idea can be disconnected from the social conflicts which create it. Today that social conflict is simple — Socialism against Capitalism, Socialist Humanism against Barbarism. The social conflict, today, is to replace Capitalism with Socialism.

The limits of Capitalist society have produced limits on the development of culture. Indeed, Capitalist society has often produced some of the most barbaric reactions against culture — in the form of war, economic crisis, social oppression, and social exploitation. The reality of the limits of Capitalist society, both for society and for culture, shows the need for a better society and a better culture. This reality shows that in the future humanity needs to develop a better society, for a better culture. This is why it is so important to develop Socialism – through the ideas of the Left and the politics of the Left.

The limits of Capitalist society have produced limits on the future of culture. Culture, today, is stuck between the limits of Capitalist society and the possibility of Socialism. Capitalism is approaching its historical limits.

Capitalism is also approaching its cultural limits. If there is any hope for a positive, human, culture in the future then it cannot be under Capitalism. It is only under Socialism that culture can be truly free, truly liberated, and truly developed.

Social struggle, in society, produces the base from which emerges culture. Since social struggle will continue to be part of human society for the foreseeable future it is likely that culture will still be shaped by social conflict and by revolutionary conflict — particularly in the form of political revolution and social revolution. This simple reality of the connection between culture and revolution means that culture will always be shaped by the social results of social struggle.

The social struggle today is very obvious. There is a simple class struggle between the capitalist class and the working class — between Capitalism and Socialism. This class struggle is evident in the realm of ideas and in the form of ideas. The struggle for Socialism is the only social struggle which really exists in society today. In the end everything, including culture, is part of that struggle.

The reality of the world today demands that people pick sides — either for Socialism or for Capitalism. Either they are on the side of Socialism — of equality, liberty, democracy, and freedom — or they are on the side of Capitalism. No person, today, can deny this political choice — even if they wish to retreat into the background of society. People cannot ignore the choice today.

We live in an age of crisis and in an age of Capitalist crisis. This period of crisis has been obvious for quite some time. It has been obvious since the emergence of Neo-Liberalism and certainly since the beginning of the crisis of 2007/2008. Art and culture cannot ignore this reality of the age of crisis — simply because the crisis is informing the world which exists around them and is changing around them. The power of this period of crisis is obvious — given the vast revolutions and counter-revolutions going on in the world at this present time. In cultural terms this means there is a great amount of raw material for society to develop cultural ideas — but it also means there is a great deal of social danger, both in the present and in the future. The political power of this age of crisis to change world society for the better is present today — in the form of Socialist Revolution and Socialism. The political power of this age of crisis to change world society for the worse is also present today — in the form of counter-revolution,

Fascism, the prospect of nuclear war and the reality of environmental crisis. No writer, writing today, can ignore the vast reality of the crisis of today. Of course, they can ignore the crisis, by writing about purely personal ideas, but that also means that their culture will be lifeless and without any real social engagement. The task of the writer is to engage with society and social reality. The task of society is to engage with society and social reality. Our present age, an age of crisis, highlights this social role of the writer. If human history continues forward (hopefully towards Socialism) the work of the writer will be vital in not only understanding those developments — but also in actually achieving the struggle to achieve Socialism. Culture cannot change the world alone — as that is the task of classes, class conflict, social revolution, and political revolution — but it can help to create intellectual revolution. Intellectual revolution is important for social revolution. Social revolution is vital for achieving Socialist revolution. In our age of crisis, the connection between culture and revolution will probably only grow.

Crisis has often produced interesting culture. This is because any social crisis forces humanity to engage with the social reality of the times, through culture. This has been a reality of the history and politics of culture since the creation of the modern world and since the first modern social revolutions. Artists, today, should not fear the crisis — except when it produces awful social results. Rather artists should try to examine and explain the crisis in order to help create a better society and a better world. The social role of culture is on full display in the connection between crisis and society. Crisis helps to push culture forward – to make better culture. Crises will come and go — but crises are crucial for pushing culture forward. Crisis forces us to change. Crisis forces us to become better.

Culture can be connected to revolution and to social revolution. Culture has always been part of the reality of revolution. Indeed, when we look at the world today, which has been in crisis since 2007/2008, we can see that some of the best culture has come out of the reality of the crisis. The world, today, is already being reshaped by social revolution. The reality of social revolution is also producing real social change – and the possibility of Socialism. Culture is part of the struggle for revolution. Culture is part of the struggle for a better society. Indeed, all of the major social struggles in the world, today, are producing revolutionary forms of culture. The most important social struggles, today, are: the struggle against Capitalism, Fascism, and Stalinism, and the struggle for Socialism. The Arab Spring, the Arab Revolution of 2010-2011, produced a great deal of revolutionary culture. Some of the best American culture, today, has come out of responses to the economic crisis of today — particularly in the form of those left-wing activists and workers who are active in social movements like Occupy and Occupy Wall Street. Some of the best British culture, in recent times, has come out of the student and worker movements of the 2010s. In Greece the best Greek writers, activists, and workers, today, have emerged in the social struggle against Capitalism and the crisis in Greece today — for the Left and for Socialism. In China, the best forms of modern Chinese culture are being produced by Chinese workers who are resisting Stalinism in China. In the Middle East, countless workers today are already struggling for a new society – as a result of the Arab Revolutions of 2010-2011. The political ability of culture to shape political expression and political struggle is something which is a real revolutionary reality today — and something which has always emerged out of periods of social crisis. Future historians and political thinkers, looking back at our times, a period of crisis, will probably argue that the culture of our times was a social response to the crisis of our times — both by the Right and by the Left. The culture produced by crisis, and by social struggle, might not always be good culture — but that culture is useful for understanding the real social crisis of our times. Culture produced in a time of crisis shows the social reality of that time. All periods of crisis produce culture. The culture of today is a result of this period of crisis. The revolutions of today might be defeated, by counter-revolution, but the words and ideas associated with those revolutions will live — and they will help to inspire future social revolutions and political revolutions. The struggle for revolution, for Socialist revolution, will always continue — until victory.

Revolution has always managed to produce good culture. At the very least revolution has produced interesting culture – culture which drives culture itself forward. This has been the case of all the great ideas which came out of the great revolutions of history — the English Revolution, the American Revolution, the French Revolution, the Revolutions of 1848, the Russian Revolution, the Chinese Revolution, the Cuban Revolution, etc. As long as social revolutions continue to develop and occur — and they will continue to develop and occur until the victory of Socialism — there will always be a real and concrete relationship between culture and revolution. Revolutions produce culture — simply as a reality of the connection between culture and revolution. Indeed, the best way that many people remember revolutions is in the form of their ideas — alongside their revolutionary results and revolutionary consequences. The history of culture is the history of the connection between culture and revolution.

Culture needs to be revolutionary today. Culture needs to be part of the revolutionary struggle to create a better world. In political terms this means that culture needs to engage with social terms and with political terms — both to develop itself and to engage with the political struggles that humanity is facing today. For Left writers, for Socialist writers, this connection between culture and revolution is already obvious. It has always been obvious from the perspective of Left writers and Socialist writers. In many ways it will always be obvious. It is only through connecting culture to revolution that culture can be truly revolutionary — becoming a force capable of inspiring the world and changing the world.

If we wish to see culture develop, both as theory and as practice, we need to develop the social forces and the social structures which can develop culture — and connect it fully to human society. Culture which becomes disconnected from human society, from human culture, from human ideas, from humanism, from humanity itself, becomes esoteric, limited, and flawed. Culture which has no basis in society or in human society loses most of its ability to connect with humanity at large. This is the death of culture as a social force. The loss of culture occurs when culture becomes no longer connected to humanity. If culture is to remain part of human culture, we must organise to ensure that culture remains part of human society — in all its cultural, social, intellectual, and political forms. The future of culture will rely on the ability of society to maintain the connection between culture, popular culture, literature, and society. A society which can no longer maintain such connections will not only lose its culture but also all of its cultural progress — which will lead to Barbarism, Fascism, and war. A society which can no longer maintain such connections will also lose its history — and the history of its culture. Humanity cannot afford to lose those elements which help to ensure social development and political development. Humanity cannot afford to lose any of the progress which it has fought so long to create and develop — which includes culture, in all its forms. Humanity cannot afford to lose its humanity. All culture is vital to the development of humanity. Culture is one of those revolutionary forces in human development. Culture is a vital part of the revolutionary forces in human development.

Socialism can, perhaps, achieve liberation for culture and for humanity. Socialism can, perhaps, lead the movement for a better culture and for a more human culture. Indeed, the history of revolutions has usually led to the expansion and liberation of culture — against the oppression of reaction. The struggle for Socialism — for an equal and co-operative society — can be helped by the struggle for a better culture and for a culture which engages with the social struggles of society. Indeed, it can be argued that Socialism is a way for culture to progress forward today — to become a better form of culture and to become better connected to human society. Capitalism, given its history and its politics, is not interested in fully developing culture. In our society, today, Capitalism considers culture only for commercial profit and therefore it only cares about profitable culture, not good culture. Indeed, Capitalism only supports culture which is profitable — which exposes the philistine nature of Capitalism. Only Socialism can fully develop a society, in modern times, where culture is both respected and socially free. Socialism can help to free culture. Culture can help Socialism to be humane and humanist.

Socialism is the key social struggle of our times. This might not seem important to culture — yet if we wish to have a society in which culture is capable of achieving its full potential then society must become Socialist. Capitalist society has no interest in culture or in artists. Capitalist society has no interest in any form of culture or literature it cannot make profit from. This means that Capitalist society will always make the development of culture difficult. Capitalist society only cares about its profits and since culture is a cultural development it is unlikely, today, that Capitalism will have much interest in the development of culture as a cultural expression. Capitalism will continue to grind down all forms of culture, including culture, until it is simply one monopoly culture which can be sold for profit and for accumulation. If culture is to have a future, as a genuine expression of human freedom and human culture, in all its various forms, it must be under Socialism — and via the political power and cultural power of Socialist culture.

Culture can be connected to Socialism. Indeed, the human basis of Socialism means that culture can emerge from Socialism and from the ideas of Socialism. Every Socialist, who is an artist, a writer, or an admirer of culture, understands this connection — and the ability of Socialism to inspire some interesting and genuine forms of culture. The task of culture, under Socialism or in the process of achieving Socialism, should be to develop itself and to achieve ever higher forms of human liberation and human expression. Culture will always be at its best when it is engaging with human society and with human reality. Socialism, a society based on co-operation and equality, cannot be anything but a human society. This means that Socialism must engage with culture, just as culture engages with Socialism.

The problems of Capitalism and Capitalist culture will not go away. The limits of Capitalist society and Capitalist culture will continue to push down on culture — until a better society emerges from Capitalism. Hopefully that better society will be a Socialist society — a society based on co-operation and equality rather than competition and hierarchy, a society based on the liberation of the working class. Socialism will free the working class from its exploitation. Socialism will free society to write. Socialism will produce a working class which will be free to develop a truly human culture — one based on co-operation and equality. Socialism will produce a culture which is truly free to write about the possibilities of culture and the hopes of society.

Culture is vital for understanding humanity. Marx understood the importance of culture for humanity and for the struggle for a better world. He understood that human culture is part of human emancipation. Indeed, Marx understood that most of the truly great examples of human culture have tended to emerge during periods of political revolution and social revolution. This view of culture and revolution shows the role of culture in the development of social revolution. The struggle for humanity, today, needs to also be a struggle for social revolution.

Culture is vital for changing the world. Christopher Caudwell, the great Marxist thinker on culture, in the 1930s, believed that there were two possibilities for the future of Culture. Either culture would remain within Capitalist society — and would be limited, forever, by the limits of Capitalist society — or culture would be part of the Socialist transformation of society and the Socialist Revolution. The choice for culture remains the same today — between Capitalism and Socialism, between Barbarism and Socialism.11

Culture is part of society. Culture cannot be separated from society. Culture can either serve the revolutions of society or the counter-revolutions of society. Indeed, culture has often served both. It is the hope of today that art and culture will serve the revolutions of society — both to free culture and to free society. The cause of revolution is the cause of humanity.12

Humanity must free itself. As Marx once said: ‘Man is the highest being for man, hence with the categorical imperative to overthrow all relations in which man is a debased, enslaved, forsaken, despicable being’.13 The goal of art is cultural freedom. The goal of revolution is human freedom.

It is only through Socialism that culture and society will be truly free — and able to produce the full potential of culture. This might seem utopian — but it is the best basis from which a truly free society might really emerge from in human terms. Culture can change society. Culture can change the world. We must struggle so that culture can help to make a Socialist world.14 We must struggle in order to achieve a free world. As William Morris, the great British Socialist, once said: "the aim of art is happiness".15

Humanity will continue to produce culture. We will continue to produce culture until humanity itself ceases to exist.16 Culture will always be part of our social struggle for a better future – a future of Socialism and freedom. In order to ensure the continuation of humanity, culture, and art, we must fight and struggle to achieve Socialism. We must struggle for revolution – as outlined by the best Socialist thinkers: Marx, Engels, Lenin, and Trotsky. Only when we have a society based on freedom can we say we live in a free, cultured, and human society.17

Notes

1. R. Luxemburg, The Crisis of German Social Democracy, (1916)
2. R. Luxemburg, The Crisis of German Social Democracy, (1916)
3. K. Marx and F. Engels, The Communist Manifesto, (1848).
4. C. Caudwell, Studies in a Dying Culture, (1938).
5. C. Caudwell, Illusion and Reality, (1937).
6. C. Caudwell, Studies in a Dying Culture, (1938).
7. C. Caudwell, Studies in a Dying Culture, (1938).
8. K. Marx and F. Engels, The Communist Manifesto, (1848).
9. C. Caudwell, Studies in a Dying Culture, (1938).
10. W. Morris, Art and Socialism, (1884)
11. C. Caudwell, Studies in a Dying Culture, (1938).
12. W. Morris, Art and Socialism, (1884)
13. K. Marx, Critique of Hegel's Philosophy of Right, (1843)
14. W. Morris, Letter on Socialism and Art, (1896)
15. W. Morris, Signs of Change, (1888)
16. R. Luxemburg, The Crisis of German Social Democracy, (1916).
17. K. Marx and F. Engels, The Communist Manifesto, (1848)

(2016)

CHAPTER IV

THE CRISIS OF CAPITALIST CULTURE – A MARXIST STUDY

This essay is a study of the crisis of Capitalist culture. Culture is the social expression of human ideas — including in times of crisis. In this essay I wish to suggest that Capitalist culture is going through a period of serious crisis. This crisis has been developing in Capitalist culture ever since the emergence of Capitalism itself. Despite its victories in the 19th century, and in the 20th century, it appears that the culture of Capitalist society, since the rise of Neo-Liberalism, is unable to overcome the serious limits and serious problems which have developed within Capitalist society since the Second World War. This crisis, in its various forms, is undermining the ability of Capitalism itself to overcome its own economic and political crises — because this crisis of culture prevents a social response to the crisis from being developed. Capitalist culture and Capitalist society, today, are connected together. The crisis of Capitalist society, today, is a crisis of Capitalist culture. The crisis of Capitalist culture, today, is a crisis of Capitalist society. The reality of this crisis is increasingly obvious in most of the main Capitalist states. Indeed, we can already feel certain aspects of this crisis of the culture of Capitalism in our everyday lives. This crisis might develop in several serious ways before it is finished — just as other major social crises and cultural crises have developed in the history of class societies. In this essay I wish to outline some of the more systematic problems of this crisis of Capitalist culture — and the effect of this crisis on Capitalist society. Perhaps this crisis will provide some of the social and cultural politics required to show the problems of Capitalism itself — and the need for Socialism. In political terms this crisis of Capitalist culture could result in either revolution or counter-revolution — as Capitalist society attempts to save itself and its culture. This essay is a Socialist essay on the crisis of Capitalist culture. It is the task of Socialists to understand Capitalism, Capitalist society, the crisis of Capitalism, and the crisis of Capitalist culture, in order to make the argument for Socialism.[1]

The Crisis

Capitalist culture, today, is in crisis. Capitalist culture is in crisis because of the overall crisis of Capitalism. A social crisis, within Capitalism, has produced a crisis of culture. This crisis is part of the overall crisis of Capitalism, today, and the tendency of Capitalism, as a system, to produce crises as part of its natural development. It is from the overall crisis of Capitalism, particularly since the emergence of Neo-Liberal Capitalism and Late Capitalism, that the crisis of Capitalist culture, in its present form, has emerged. The crisis is defined by the overall alienation of humanity from the culture being produced, today, by Capitalism. The crisis is not an outlier of the Capitalist system — but a vital and historical part of it. Capitalist culture is in crisis because the Capitalist system cannot overcome its overall social crisis — which is part of the overall nature of Capitalism. Indeed, the crisis of Capitalism, today, highlights part of the overall crisis of Capitalism itself, both as an economic system and as a social system. It is important to recognise that 'crisis' does not always mean 'decline'. Capitalist culture exists today — and it exists strongly, today, as the most powerful form of culture in the world today — yet it is clearly also in crisis. The full effect of Capitalist culture can be seen in the fact that it exists in all forms of modern mass culture — and on a huge scale. The crisis of Capitalist culture is not a crisis of ideas, quality, or quantity — but rather a crisis of contradictions, a crisis of alienation, and a crisis of monopoly. The crisis of Capitalist culture has been caused by the crisis of Capitalism itself. Capitalist culture is in crisis, despite its power, its scale, its quantity, and its quality, because of the overall crisis of Capitalism itself. Capitalist culture has many problems and many contradictions — which has produced the crisis in Capitalist culture. The crisis of Capitalist culture is not simply a crisis of culture, but rather it is part of a social crisis and an economic crisis. It is a crisis of culture and ideas, and a crisis of society and economics. Capitalism is the source of a number of the inhumane problems of our current culture. The result is humanity is facing the inhumanity of Capitalism.2 Humanity must overcome inhumanity.

The Nature of the Crisis

In this section of the essay, we can discuss the nature of the crisis. Capitalism, today, has clearly been in crisis since the crisis of 2008. The fundamental nature of this crisis is social — it has social origins, and it has social consequences. We cannot understand the problems of Capitalist culture by just looking at the cultural reality of Capitalism today. We need to look at the deeper developments of Capitalism today — of how it generates its culture and how it generates its ideas. We seriously need to do this in order to really confront the cultural and social problems of our times — and to solve them in a humane and effective way. Much of our ability to solve the crisis of Capitalist culture, as well as wider social problems, will probably depend on our social and political ability to really understand the nature of Capitalism itself — especially its basis in exploitation and oppression. Much of our ability to really solve the crisis of Capitalist culture will depend on our ability to overcome Capitalism itself — by establishing Socialism and a Socialist society.

The crisis of Capitalist culture, today, is a crisis of Neo-Liberalism. Specifically, it is a crisis of both the society of Neo-Liberalism and the culture of Neo-Liberalism. Neo-Liberalism, as it has emerged from the 1970s and 1980s, has created a world culture — but it has also reinforced the basic problems of Capitalism and Capitalist culture. Neo-Liberalism, as a form of Capitalism, based on privatisation and finance, was the attempt to save Capitalism from its problems in the 1960s and 1970s — which included the problems of its culture at that time. Neo-Liberalism solved the problems of Capitalism and Capitalist culture, in the 1980s and 1990s, by the means of a counter-revolution against the working class, the privatisation of society, and the unleashing of the 'free market'. In the area of society and economics we already know how much of a disaster this has been over the last few decades. Neo-Liberalism has also been a disaster for culture — because it has limited human culture to just Capitalist ideas. Instead of placing culture in the hands of all, Neo-Liberalism has placed culture in the hands of those few capitalists who control the means of producing culture — particularly in the area of mass media. Neo-Liberalism also only wants profit — and it only produces culture which is profitable. The overall effect of Neo-Liberalism on culture has been privatisation, monopolisation, concentration, de-humanisation, and domination of culture by Capitalism. If we really believe in culture, the ability of culture to improve and liberate humanity, then we also know that the effect of Neo-Liberalism, upon culture and humanity, has been a disaster.

The crisis of Capitalist culture is a fatal crisis. Capitalism has had other crises in its history — and it has been able to overcome them — but it cannot overcome all of its crises forever. Eventually the crises of Capitalism, including the cultural crisis of today, will prove fatal. Capitalism, eventually, will fall and be replaced by something else, hopefully Socialism. Indeed, it is not the cultural problems of Capitalism which ultimately undermine

Capitalism — but its economic problems and its social problems. Capitalism, eventually, will find a solution to its cultural crisis — by developing new forms of Neo-Liberal culture — but Capitalism cannot solve the deeper economic crisis which is unfolding today. It is the economic crisis of Capitalism, in the end, which shows the limits and the problems of Capitalism itself. It is the economic problems, political problems, social problems, and environmental problems of Capitalism, which will eventually end Capitalism itself — and hopefully replace it with Socialism. The crisis of Capitalist culture remains important, and we must understand it, but the deeper crisis of Capitalism is economic, and it is social. Socialism will, hopefully, solve all the crises of Capitalism — by abolishing it and by finally overthrowing it.3

The Origins of the Crisis

In this section of the essay, we can discuss the origins of the crisis, and how it relates to the broader crisis of Capitalism.

The origins of the crisis of Capitalist culture lie in Capitalism itself. Capitalism, as a system, is built on crisis — and it consistently produces crisis and goes into crisis. To understand the origins of the current crisis of Capitalist culture is to understand the reality of the crisis of Capitalism. The current crisis of Capitalism, since 2007/2008, is reflective of the overall nature of Capitalism — the tendency of Capitalism to produce crisis, and the tendency of Capitalism itself to go into crisis. All of the economic, social, political, intellectual, and cultural crises of Capitalism, both in the past and today, show that Capitalism has a historical tendency of producing crisis — as an inherent and inevitable part of Capitalism itself. The current crisis of Capitalist culture is the product of the current crisis of Capitalism. The current crisis of Capitalism is the product of the historical tendency of Capitalism to produce crisis. The origins of the crisis of today lie in the crises of the past.4

The crisis of Capitalist culture, today, is a result of Neo-Liberalism. Neo-Liberal Capitalism, today, is in crisis. It has, clearly, been in crisis since 2007/2008. As a result, Neo-Liberal culture is also in crisis. This basic fact should be clear if we look at the majority of the Capitalist world and the majority of the states in the Capitalist world which are in crisis — particularly in Europe, the United States, Latin America, and the Middle East. If we really are to understand the current crisis, we need to engage with the reality of Neo-Liberalism itself — as an economic system, as a political system, as a social system, and as a cultural system. It is on this basis that we can really engage with the current crisis — both in intellectual terms and political terms. Neo-Liberalism, as a system, was designed to solve the deeper problems of Capitalism in the 1970s and 1980s. For a long period, the 1980s, 1990s, and the 2000s, Neo-Liberalism managed to solve these problems — but it has also generated a much deeper crisis for Capitalism itself. The current crisis of Capitalist culture is a result of the wider crisis of Neo-Liberalism.5

The Politics of the Crisis

In this section of the essay, we can discuss some of the politics of the crisis of Capitalist culture.

1. The crisis that is affecting Capitalism, today, is a difficult crisis to understand. We can all see the economic, political, social, and intellectual results of the crisis — but we have yet to really see the cultural results of the crisis. Capitalism, economically, can see that it is in crisis, but Capitalism, culturally, cannot see that it is in crisis. This fact might have major results for Capitalism — because societies which cannot solve their economic, political, social, intellectual, and cultural problems tend to enter periods of social revolution. A major social result of the crisis of Capitalism, today, is that it could result in a new period of social revolution — in a new period of Socialist Revolution.

2. The crisis of Capitalist culture has resulted in a society which is feeling the reality of crisis itself — in terms of economics, society, politics, ideas, and culture. This means that the crisis of Capitalist culture is part of a broader crisis — the crisis of Capitalism.

3. The full effects of the current crisis of Capitalist culture cannot be fully outlined — as the crisis is still developing. The point, here, is the need to think about some of the social results of the current crisis — showing the reality of the effects of the crisis of Capitalist culture on the culture of humanity. We are living in a period of crisis — and we can see and feel this crisis in all parts of our lives, and in all parts of our cultures.

4. The crisis has affected society. This can be seen in the way that social culture has reacted to the crisis. In most societies, especially in the Capitalist states, society has reacted to the crisis by attacking culture itself. Most reactionaries, today, blame culture, or 'bad culture', for the current crisis.

This has become an increasing part of Capitalist politics since 2007 — especially on the Right. The Right, today, blames all the problems of Capitalism and Capitalist society not on the problems of Capitalism itself — but instead blames all of society.

5. The crisis has affected the working class. The working class has always developed its own culture — in order to humanise itself and to ensure the self-liberation of itself. Under Capitalism, and under the current crisis of Capitalism, the culture of the working class has always been attacked and undermined — especially when that culture offers opposition to Capitalism and to the culture of Capitalism. As the working class struggles, today, in order to free itself, it always develops its own culture — and its own sense of community and culture. This culture is universal and internationalist. This culture, this working-class culture, is vital to building a Socialist culture. The crisis of Capitalism, such as the crisis of Capitalism today, threatens to always undermine the culture of the working class. If the working class wishes to be free and to be emancipated, if it wishes to build its own culture and its own Socialism, it must resist Capitalism in all ways and in all forms. This struggle, hopefully, will lead, in part, to Socialism. Today, with the current lack of an effective struggle for Socialism, we can see the full results of the crisis of Capitalism for the culture of the working class — as Capitalism attempts, constantly, to attack the culture of the working class and to smash the culture of the working class. The crisis of Capitalist culture is a direct attack on the culture of the working class.

6. The crisis has affected individuals. Individuals, across the world, can see the reality of the crisis of Capitalist culture. These same individuals experience and feel the reality of the crisis of Capitalist culture. These individuals, mostly workers, feel and experience alienation every year, every month, and every day, of their lives, due to the reality of Capitalism. This alienation is reinforced, again and again, by the reality of Capitalist culture. Most of the time these individual workers suffer in silence — as they attempt to live their lives and as they attempt to build their communities. Despite this these individuals, when organised as workers, can sometimes overcome the alienation of Capitalism and Capitalist culture. By struggling against the alienation of Capitalist society these workers can often find ways of building a new society and a new culture. The experience of class struggle and the experience of revolution, in the real world, can often help in overcoming the reality of Capitalism and Capitalist culture. Indeed, it is the struggle of these workers, when organised into unions or parties, which has provided the only examples of workers overcoming their alienation — and

the alienation of the crisis of Capitalist culture. As we struggle against the reality of the crisis of Capitalism and the crisis of Capitalist culture it is often these workers, in their millions, who provide the best way to overcome both the crisis and Capitalism itself. Hopefully, in the near future, these workers will succeed in overcoming Capitalism completely. Their struggle will not only overcome Capitalism, and alienation, but it might just bring into existence a new form of society and a new form of culture — the society of Socialism and the culture of Socialism.

7. One of the worst aspects of the crisis of Capitalist culture is its effects on ordinary people. Due to the fact that Capitalism has monopolised culture, and concentrated culture, it has resulted in a cultural society where most workers have few ways of accessing culture — or the benefits of culture. Most workers, due to their exploitation and their alienation, have few chances to fully experience the full potential of culture — or their own potential to take part in the development of culture.

8. The crisis has affected politics. Indeed, the crisis has shown the necessity of Socialism. This is clear if we look at how many humans, today, react to both politics, society, and culture. There is a sense, today, in many societies, that Capitalist society is in the middle of some form of transformation — a crisis with no clear result yet. Most of humanity, today, can see that the economic crisis of Neo-Liberalism has transformed into a social crisis — a social crisis with cultural elements and a cultural crisis of society and culture. The general sense of alienation, common in most Capitalist societies, has only increased in the last few decades, leaving behind a massive increase in the general sense of despair and alienation felt by millions and millions of people. Indeed, billions now feel a sense of alienation under Capitalist society. Capitalism, in social terms, has clearly run out of momentum — just as it did in the 1930s and in the 1970s. Today, in order to solve the overall sense of crisis being felt by humanity we need to seriously consider both the crisis of Capitalism and the possibility of Socialism. In political terms and cultural terms, humanity needs to debate its options in the coming century — and hopefully seek to build a new and better society. It is only when humanity has overcome the crisis of exploitation and oppression — which produces the ultimate form of crisis — that humanity, at last, can call itself free. The emancipation of humanity depends on the emancipation of humanity from Capitalism. Only Socialism can emancipate humanity from Capitalism. Only Socialism can bring about the end of the crisis of Capitalism.

The Results of the Crisis

In this section of the essay, we might briefly consider some of the results of the crisis of Capitalist culture.

It is too early, yet, to understand all the results of the current crisis of Capitalism — and the current crisis of Capitalist culture. What can be said, however, is that the crisis is far from resolved.

1. In economic terms the crisis of Capitalist culture highlights the full problems of Neo-Liberalism — in economic terms, social terms, and cultural terms.

2. In political terms the crisis of Capitalist culture highlights the political problems of Capitalism – its political inability to solve the crisis.

3. In social terms the crisis of Capitalist culture shows that Capitalism is suffering a serious social crisis — a crisis with economic problems, social problems, political problems, and cultural problems.

4. In intellectual terms the crisis of Capitalist culture shows that Capitalism has no new ideas — and has had no new ideas since the rise of Neo-Liberalism in the 1970s and the 1980s, nearly a half-century ago.

5. All class societies tend to generate crises and problems. All class societies also tend to generate crises of culture. Feudal society produced crises of Feudal culture. Capitalist society, today, is producing its own crisis of culture. In order to really overcome the crisis of culture, today, we need to overcome class society itself. We need to establish a society which abolishes class and class society — in the form of Socialism.

6. In basic social terms the crisis of Capitalist culture highlights that Capitalism, as a culture, is bankrupt — and needs to be replaced by Socialism and by Socialist Humanism.

Culture, History, and Capitalism

The crisis of Capitalist culture needs to be understood as a historical crisis. The crisis of Capitalist culture is part of the crisis of Capitalism. Indeed, the overall problems of Capitalist culture have been obvious since the beginning of Capitalist society. The crisis has historical roots and historical origins —

within the very nature of Capitalism as a social and historical system. Every serious crisis of the Capitalist system, since the origins of Capitalism, has produced a cultural crisis, alongside an economic crisis and a social crisis. Indeed, this cultural crisis has been obvious since the latter half of the 19th century and since the beginning of the 20th century. From the 1870s to the outbreak of the First World War, in 1914, the confidence of Capitalist culture began to experience its first crisis — its first great crisis since the victory of Capitalism over Feudalism. The origins of the crisis of Capitalist culture have their own historical origins here — in the breakdown of 19th century society, 19th century culture, and the outbreak of the First World War. The outbreak of the First World War and the victory of the October Revolution showed that Capitalism was possibly not eternal — that it might be replaced by something else. The crisis of the Great Depression, the rise of Fascism and Nazism, and the results of the Second World War, also showed that Capitalist culture and Capitalist society were capable of Barbarism, which also reinforced the crisis of Capitalist culture. Despite the end of the 20th century, and the victory of Neo-Liberalism, Capitalism, today, still feels the results of the breakdown of Capitalist society itself after 1914. The struggle for Socialism, even today, shows that Capitalism and Capitalist culture might yet be replaced by something else — by Socialism. This crisis of Capitalist culture has stayed with Capitalism since 1914 — even into the post-war period of Capitalist culture after 1945 and after 1991. Capitalism, today, while surviving the great wars and great revolutions of the 20th century, still feels the reality and the impact of the crisis of Capitalist culture. Capitalism, today, has a major form of culture — but it has never been able to recover the confidence which it once had in the 19th century. While Capitalism has managed to survive and develop, up to this current point of history, today, it still suffers from the serious problems and serious crises which have impacted it since the late 19th century. Every major crisis of Capitalism — in the 19th century, in the 20th century, in the Great Depression, in the crisis of the 1970s, in the crisis of 2008-2009 — has impacted the culture of Capitalism and the confidence of the culture of Capitalism. If we are to ever understand the crisis of Capitalist culture, today, we must understand its connection to the historical crises of Capitalism — particularly in the last two centuries. Capitalism, as a historical system, produces social crises and economic crises. The crises of Capitalism also produce crises of culture and the development of culture. The culture of Capitalism, in its development and its structure, has always had to adapt to the reality of the crisis of Capitalism itself. The culture of Capitalism, even today, is the historical product of the result of the crisis. So long as Capitalism exists it will continue to produce crises. So long as

Capitalism exists it will continue to produce crises for the culture of Capitalism. The crisis of Capitalist culture is part of the historical crisis of Capitalism itself.6

The Crisis and Monopoly

A key part of the crisis of Capitalist culture is the reality of the monopoly of Capitalist culture. Indeed, the fact that Capitalism produces monopolies, and monopolisation, in general, means that it also produces a monopolisation of culture. Under Capitalism we have seen a centralisation of culture and a monopolisation of culture — with fewer and fewer outlets of cultural production. Culture, today, is now increasingly produced and controlled by smaller and smaller Capitalist companies, who control more and more of the means of producing culture. While Capitalism, today, boasts of the increasing means to develop and consume culture, at a greater rate than ever before in human history, the reality is that most people live and experience their culture from fewer and fewer sources. The majority of film, print, media, music, art, social culture, personal culture, human culture, and other forms of culture exist within the system of Capitalism — and within the monopolisation of Capitalism. As Capitalism has developed it has become more and more concentrated, more and more monopolised, and its culture is more concentrated and more monopolised. This is true of Capitalist culture too. A major criticism of Capitalist culture has to be based on this tendency within Capitalist culture — the tendency towards monopoly and concentration. A culture which is monopolised and concentrated is not a free culture.

Culture is commodified and branded under Capitalism. This is the reality of culture under Capitalism. It is also the result of the crisis of culture under Capitalism. The end result of all this development of the reality of culture under Capitalism is the crisis of culture and the crisis of Society. Where culture is commodified — so too is humanity. This result cannot be seen as good for culture — or good for humanity.7

The Crisis and Alienation

The crisis of Capitalist culture is a universal crisis. It clearly exists in all societies, and in all states, today. Almost all human beings, in the world, today, are affected by the crisis. This means that the crisis is connected to human alienation. The crisis exists in all Capitalist societies and all Capitalist states — to one extent or another. Indeed, a key fact of the crisis of Capitalist culture is that it shows how much of the current crisis of Capitalism is based on alienation — on the alienation of workers and people from culture, from society, from humanity, and from themselves. The crisis can be seen and felt in all parts of the world — especially those societies which have gone through a period of social crisis and political crisis since the 2000s — especially since the crisis of 2007/2008. We cannot limit the crisis to a particular society or a particular culture — because it exists in all societies which are based on Capitalism or linked to Capitalism, especially in the form of Neo-Liberal Capitalism. This means that the crisis is total, and the crisis is universal. It exists in every part of the globe and in nearly every society in the world. In many ways the height of the crisis of Capitalist culture is the crisis of alienation itself. Humanity, today, is feeling the full effects of alienation. Humanity has under-estimated the power and the results of alienation — resulting in a society based on alienation and the reality of Capitalist alienation. The crisis of culture is both a cultural crisis, and a social crisis: a crisis of alienation.

Capitalist culture, concentrated into fewer and fewer hands, has resulted in a monopolisation of the means to create culture. This reality is central to the cultural crisis of Capitalism. The workers, as a result, have fewer and fewer opportunities to create culture or to enjoy culture. This has reinforced the reality of alienation in Capitalism — continuing to isolate millions of workers from their humanity and their right to a cultured life. Indeed, Capitalism alienates workers as much as it exploits workers — in the barbaric reality of Capitalism itself. The result, today, is a major part of the crisis of Capitalist culture — and a major part of the cultural alienation of the working class.8

The Crisis and Barbarism

We need to remember that Capitalism will always seek to maintain itself — at the expense of humanity. This means that Capitalism will often try to use Barbarism to resolve its crises — including its crises of culture. The history of Fascism, and the politics of Fascism, show that Capitalism is prepared to use the most inhuman methods and the most inhumane means to maintain itself. Fascism is the most reactionary form of Capitalism — it is Capitalism during periods of crisis. Fascism is the most reactionary form of (modern) class society. The decay of Capitalism, and the decay of the culture of Capitalism, has led to the rise of Fascism in human history — in the 1920s, the 1930s, and the 1940s. Fascism, as a reactionary middle-class movement, is designed to maintain Capitalism. Fascism, as the most reactionary form of Capitalism, is designed to maintain Capitalism, through the methods of Barbarism. Capitalism and its culture might attempt to use Fascism again — during the current crisis of Capitalism.

Capitalism, itself, today, is in crisis. This means that Capitalism has to face both its own problems and the problems of its culture. While Capitalism, so far, has failed to address the current crisis — and the current crisis of culture — it will eventually have to look at the reality of the crisis, and find solutions. Capitalism has a history of crisis and although it has usually failed to fully solve any of its crises, Capitalism does have a history of finding temporary solutions to its problems — before generating new and deeper crises. The history of both the 19th century and the 20th century, the height of Capitalism, is full of examples of how Capitalism has attempted to solve its crises and its problems — including the crises of its culture. Sometimes this has led to some of the best years of Capitalist society and Capitalist culture — such as the period before the First World War or the long boom after the Second World War. Most of the time, however, Capitalism has always tried to use barbarism as a means of solving its problems — such as the Napoleonic Wars, the Depression of the 19th century, Imperialism in both the 19th century and the 20th century, the First World War, the Second World War, Fascism, Nazism, and genocide. Capitalism, because it cannot overcome the central problems of its mode of production, has to rely on barbarism in order to avoid these problems. Much of the barbarism of human culture and human society, in the last few centuries, can be attributed towards the means by which Capitalism saves its own system from its own problems. Culture is used in this process — to justify barbarism, to justify war, to justify imperialism, and to justify genocide. Capitalism has used culture to elevate and to develop its own system — but it has also used culture to maintain and to justify its crimes. If we really want to understand the possible results of the crisis of Capitalist culture, we need to place those results within the historical development of Capitalism itself — with all its crises, all its problems, and all its uses of barbarism to maintain itself. Since Capitalism, today, is in crisis, it is likely that Capitalism might use the same solutions to solve its deeper economic problems and political problems — including its cultural problems. Capitalism, in the end, might return to Barbarism and to Fascism.

Capitalism, in crisis, produces reaction. Reaction, in the end, produces Fascism. The threat of Fascism is the ultimate threat of Capitalism and of Capitalist culture to human society, specifically when Capitalism fails to solve its crises. Fascism is the most reactionary form of Capitalism – a dictatorship of the most reactionary sections of Capitalism. We must be aware of this threat as we move into the future. Capitalism is perfectly capable of using dictatorship and Fascism to save itself and its culture, in times of crisis, such as today. It has already done this once before in history — in the reality of Fascism and the reality of Nazism. We cannot allow this to occur again. The society of Capitalism must not be allowed to be replaced by the society of Fascism. We must resist Fascism at all cost.

The problem of the crisis of Capitalist culture is the possibility that its crisis will reinforce the existing crisis of Capitalism — resulting in war and conflict. The history of Capitalism, after all, is the history of war, conflict, imperialism, and dictatorship — at least in times of crisis. We currently live in an era of crisis and a period of crisis. We need to be aware of this as we struggle to confront the crisis and as we struggle to find a human solution to the crisis. The only solution, the only human solution, to the crisis of Capitalism, is a Socialist solution — the solution of Socialism. If humanity is to ever emerge from the current crisis of Capitalism, and the current crisis of Capitalist culture, it will have to be via Socialism.9

The Crisis and Late Capitalism

The crisis shows the reality of culture under Late Capitalism — Capitalism since the 1980s. This reality is that Capitalism produces a culture of alienation and a culture of inhumanity. The reality of war, conflict, famine, despair, genocide, exploitation, and oppression, caused by Capitalism, in modern times, underlines the fact that Capitalism is incapable of producing a human culture or a humanist culture. The logic of this is quite clear in social terms and political terms — in order to overcome the crisis of Capitalist culture we must overcome Capitalism itself. In order to overcome Capitalism, we must overthrow it — and replace it with a society based on human liberation and human emancipation, in the form of Socialism.

Capitalism commercialises all aspects of life — for profit and for accumulation. Capitalism also alienates humanity from culture. This is clearly the case if we apply this to culture. Capitalism has always commercialised culture — and this process is only speeding up during the Neo-Liberal period of Capitalism. The economic imperative of culture, under Capitalism, is profit and will always be profit. This means that culture, under Capitalism, will always be shaped by the economic imperative for profit. This vision of culture and art means that culture and art will always be degraded, over time, by Capitalism — in order to generate profit.

Capitalism, in the end, will always result in a hollowed-out culture and a hollowed-out society.10

The Crisis and the Nature of Capitalism

One of the key results of the crisis is that it shows the overall nature of the crisis of Capitalism itself. The crisis of culture shows that Capitalism is undergoing a total crisis, a general crisis. This crisis is affecting all parts of Capitalism and all parts of Capitalist society — from top to bottom, from economics to politics, from society to culture. The economic nature of the crisis, since 2008, has also confirmed the social and cultural nature of the crisis — leading to the overall crisis of Capitalism. The crisis of Capitalist culture can only be really understood as part of the crisis of Capitalism itself.11

That the crisis of Capitalism is affecting the culture of Capitalism should be obvious. Every culture, in history, has been shaped by the wider society which produced it. A crisis of society produces a crisis of culture. No culture, in the end, can escape the economic base which created it or the economic crises which emerge from that economic base — as culture is, in the end, part of the social superstructure and not the economic base of society. Capitalist culture is, ultimately, affected by the wider society of Capitalism. The crisis of one affects the other. What is surprising, today, is the inability of Capitalist culture to develop any real response to its own crisis — or the general crisis of Capitalism itself. In history, most cultures tend to react to the crises of their social systems. Today's Capitalist culture is not really responding to the crisis of Capitalism — rather it is ignoring it and pretending as if the wider crisis does not exist. Capitalist culture is surrounded by crisis and yet it seems to be ignoring the reality of the crisis. This odd situation is probably a result of the fact that Capitalism, and Capitalist culture, was so confident, in the 1980s and 1990s, that upon being faced with the new crisis of today the entire system really cannot acknowledge that it is facing a period of difficulty and crisis. The crisis of Capitalism is so general and so total, today, that even the culture of Capitalism cannot really engage with the reality of the crisis. The crisis is so total that the culture of Capitalism cannot effectively respond to it. This means that in the long run the culture of Capitalism probably has no real future. A culture which cannot recognise its own crisis is a culture which will, inevitably, fall apart. This does not mean that Capitalism will fall apart — but it does mean that the current structure of the culture of Capitalism, as it has existed since the 1980s, will probably face a terminal crisis, just as the

Capitalist culture of the 1890s collapsed in the First World War, just as the Capitalist culture of the 1950s collapsed in the Social Revolutions of the 1960s. If Capitalism is to survive the coming period, it will have to change its culture in one way or another — beyond the limits of Neo-Liberalism. Hopefully, something better than that will emerge — hopefully, Socialism. Hopefully, Democratic Socialism will emerge from the current crisis of Capitalism.12 The crisis of Capitalism and the crisis of Capitalist culture shows the need for Socialism — and the potential for Socialism.13

Culture and Humanity

Culture is about improving humanity. Culture is about humanity improving itself. It is about developing the ideas, principles, art, literature, and concepts, which are needed to liberate humanity. Culture should be about humanity uniting in itself — and respecting all the various parts of human society and human culture which make up humanity as a whole. The goal of culture should be a human society and a humanised society. The goal of culture should be about humanism, hopefully even Socialist Humanism. Culture is about giving humanity the means to think about itself, its society, its ideas, its environment, its past, and its future. Culture should be about unifying humanity, in all its parts, and giving it both distinct cultures and a universal culture. Culture, in the end, should be the best part of humanity — our ability to work towards improving each of us, and all of us. Capitalist culture, in its long history, has been part of that process of human improvement and human liberation — but its time as a revolutionary form of culture is over. It has been over for a century — ever since it plunged the world into the misery of the First World War, the Second World War, and the Cold War. Capitalism is also responsible for producing some of the most horrific turns to barbarism in the history of humanity. Humanity's barbarism towards humanity was one result of the barbarism of Capitalism and Capitalist culture during the dreadful 20th century.14 Capitalism is fully capable of producing wonderful culture alongside the most horrific forms of barbarism.15 Indeed, the same society which produced the beauty of the belle epoque of the 1870s, 1880s, 1890s, and 1900s also went on to produce the reality of poison gas and the mud of the trenches in the First World War. The wonderful culture of German Civilisation did not prevent the Nazis from leading the world into the horrors of the Second World War and the Holocaust. It is time, in the early 21st century, to think about the means by which we, as a human species, might move beyond the limits of Capitalism and Capitalist culture — towards a new culture and a new form of life. Humanity needs to move forward, in history, in politics, and in society, in order to develop itself — in order to liberate itself.16 Humanity cannot allow itself to be consistently held back in earlier stages of culture — specifically forms of culture based on greed, inhumanity, and barbarism. Humanity needs to move forward — to create a culture based on co-operation, solidarity, respect, and humanity. It seems that Capitalism and Capitalist culture cannot create such a culture — an actual human culture. It also seems that Capitalism and Capitalist culture are in such a crisis that they cannot even move beyond the limits of our current period in history. It is time to move forward, beyond the crisis and beyond the inhumanity, and towards a new society and a new culture — a liberated culture, a Socialist culture, a liberated society, a Socialist society. Culture belongs to each, and culture belongs to all. As Marx said, the only way to have a liberated society is to have a liberated humanity.17

The Crisis and Politics

The crisis of Capitalist culture is a global crisis. In order to confront it we will need global solutions. We need global solutions for a global culture — for humanity and for a human culture. In order to overcome Capitalism itself we will need global solutions. This means that we will have to develop political solutions — both to the general crisis of Capitalism, and the cultural crisis of Capitalism. This also means that the current crisis will generate political conflict between the Right and the Left — over the crisis, over culture, over politics, and over the future. This global reality of the crisis reinforces the global need for Socialism. If we are to achieve a solution to the international problems of Capitalism and Capitalist culture, we will need the international solutions of Socialism and Socialist culture. This is the logical, revolutionary, reality of the crisis. Hopefully, humanity will be able to solve this crisis — with Socialism and with Humanity.18

The Crisis and the Right

The crisis is a result of the politics and problems of Capitalism. It is also a result of the failure of the Right, since the 1970s, to overcome the problems of Capitalist society. The Right has been in power, in most societies and most states, since the 1980s and 1990s, since the rise of Neo-Liberalism and since the collapse of the Soviet Union and the Eastern bloc in 1989-1991, and yet the Right, somehow, cannot accept that it has caused the crisis of society today — despite having all the power, in most societies and states, since the 1980s. The Right has caused the crisis of today — and yet the Right cannot accept its responsibility of having caused the crisis. Indeed, the Right is in power, in most countries, today, and yet it acts as if the current crisis is not its fault or its responsibility. This means that, fundamentally, the Right has no solution to the crisis of today — except to repeat the failures of the past four decades.

The Crisis and the Left

The Left must try to understand the crisis of Capitalist culture. Some of the best Left writing on Capitalism has come from trying to understand the effect of Capitalism on culture. The current crisis, because it is a crisis, highlights some of the best Left analysis of Capitalism and culture today. We may not be able to completely understand the nature of the current crisis, but we can understand that it is affecting culture and society. A Left response to the crisis is needed — hopefully, a Socialist response. The Left needs to understand the crisis of Capitalist culture alongside the crisis of Capitalism. This is a key task for Left analysis of the crisis of Capitalism as it exists today. If we understand the cultural crisis, alongside the economic crisis and the political crisis, we will have a better understanding of the crisis of Capitalism. The Left also has the opportunity, today, to advance the struggle for Socialism while also trying to avoid the economic, social, and historical problems of Socialism in the 20th century (e.g. Stalinism). The Left has a chance, today, to struggle for a better world — if it can understand the crisis.

Solutions to the Crisis

We can conclude this essay by briefly discussing some of the solutions to the crisis of Capitalist culture. Are there any solutions to these problems or this crisis? Of course, the Capitalist system, as it has always done, will try to find solutions and answers to the current crisis. This essay, as a Left essay, believes that the only solution to the crisis of Capitalism is the solution of Socialism. Only Socialism, a society based on solidarity and co-operation, can overcome the crisis of Capitalism — because it will abolish Capitalism and abolish Class Society. The only human solution to the problems of the culture of Capitalism is to abolish Capitalism itself — to create a new society and a new culture, a new human society, and a new human culture. Capitalist society, and Capitalist culture, has lived out its historical role and its social role — in developing human society to our current period in history. It is time to move beyond the problems of Capitalist society and Capitalist culture — and to build a better society and a better culture. Only Socialism can create a society and a culture which is based on the humanity of all humans — and the freedom of all humans.19

The results of the crisis of Capitalist culture can be seen all over the world. Capitalism is clearly incapable of solving its economic, political, social, intellectual, and ecological problems — and as a result it cannot solve its cultural problems. Alienation is a fundamental reality of Capitalism, and its culture.20 Capitalism today is entering a period of a cultural wasteland — incapable of recognising the problem, let alone solving the problem. The overconfidence of Capitalism, and the capitalist class, in the last thirty years, since the rise of Neo-Liberalism, has meant that Capitalism itself cannot recognise its problems or come up with solutions to them. Societies which cannot recognise their problems or solve their problems inevitably change — and they are changed by revolution. The possibility which emerges from the crisis of Capitalist culture is a revolutionary possibility for change. It is a possibility that Capitalism itself will be overthrown and replaced by a better society. Hopefully that better society, with a better culture, will be a Socialist society.21 A Socialist society would solve not only the economic and political problems of Capitalist society, but it would also solve a key problem of world society today — the problems of Capitalist culture.22 Through solving the problems of culture we might produce some solutions for the problems of humanity, and create a free, equal, and better world.

Notes

1. K. Marx, Capital Vol. I, (1867)
2. C. Caudwell, Studies in a Dying Culture, (1938)
3. D. Harvey, A Short History of Neo-Liberalism, (2005)
4. C. Caudwell, Studies in a Dying Culture, (1938)
5. M. Berman, All That Is Solid Melts Into Air, (1982)
6. C. Caudwell, Studies in a Dying Culture, (1938)
7. M. Fischer, Capitalist Realism, (2009)
8. C. Caudwell, Studies in a Dying Culture, (1938)
9. E.P. Thompson, Socialist Humanism, (1957)
10. K. Marx, Capital Vol. I, (1867)
11. F. Engels, Socialism: Utopian and Scientific, (1880)
12. K. Marx, Economic and Philosophical Manuscripts of 1844, (1844)
13. E.P. Thompson, Socialist Humanism, (1957)
14. E.P. Thompson, Socialist Humanism, (1957)
15. E.P. Thompson, Socialist Humanism, (1957)
16. K. Marx, Economic and Philosophical Manuscripts of 1844, (1844)
17. E.P. Thompson, Socialist Humanism, (1957)
18. E.P. Thompson, Socialist Humanism, (1957)
19. B. Ollman, Alienation, (1971)

20. E.P. Thompson, Socialist Humanism, (1957)
21. E.P. Thompson, Socialist Humanism, (1957)
22. E.P. Thompson, Socialist Humanism, (1957)

(2014)

CHAPTER V

CAPITALIST CULTURE – HISTORY AND POLITICS

This short essay is a study of the history and politics of Capitalist culture. Capitalist culture is that culture which has emerged to justify the economics, politics, history, and ideas of Capitalism. Since the 1500s, the 1600s, the 1700s, and the 1800s, Capitalism has developed its own culture and its own visions of culture. This culture serves to both reinforce Capitalism and to develop Capitalism. This means that Capitalist culture, like all culture, has a history and a politics. The history of Capitalist culture is well developed — going back to the origins of Capitalism and the origins of the transition from Feudalism to Capitalism (1450-1850). The politics of Capitalist culture is also well developed — creating a cultural basis to the main politics of Capitalism and Capitalist society, in the form of Liberalism, Conservatism, and Fascism. This essay is a Socialist essay on the history and politics of Capitalist culture. As a result, this essay is a critical essay of both the history and politics of Capitalist culture.

The history of Capitalism outlines the history of Capitalist culture. Capitalist culture emerged with the development of Capitalism. Capitalism, the system of wage-labour and accumulation, began in Europe in the 1500s, the 1600s, the 1700s, and the 1800s. Specifically every major Capitalist Revolution, from the Renaissance to today, from the American Revolution to the French Revolution, has used culture to develop the ideological basis of Capitalism. Capitalist culture, in historical terms, emerged because of the economic, social, political, and cultural development of Capitalism.

Capitalism was a revolutionary development — as it emerged out of Feudalism in the 1400s, the 1500s, the 1600s, the 1700s, and the 1800s. The long revolutions which produced Capitalism produced a revolutionary development — the economics, politics, society, and culture of Capitalism. Capitalist culture, the culture of today, is the ultimate result of the revolutions which produced Capitalism. In many ways the culture of

Capitalism is the culture which has been produced by the long history of Capitalism.

We, today, live in the realities of Capitalism. We live in a Capitalist society. We live in a Capitalist culture. The social struggle, today, however, is the struggle to transition from Capitalism to Socialism. This is because Capitalism is no longer a revolutionary force. The only really revolutionary force in the world, today, is Socialism.

The politics of Capitalism outlines the politics of Capitalist culture. In political terms, Capitalist culture helps to promote and to defend the economic reality of Capitalism — by providing it with a cultural system and a cultural arm. The development of Capitalism, since the 1500s, has used culture to promote the overall development of Capitalism itself. This connection ensures that the cultural development of humanity, since at least the 1500s, has been shaped by the economic development of Capitalism. The cultural development of Capitalism is connected to the political development of Capitalism.

The emergence of a Capitalist culture probably began with the slow transition from Feudalism — beginning with the crisis of Feudalism. The crisis of the 14th century, in Western Europe, led to the eventual breakdown of both Feudal society and Feudal culture. The revolutions of the Renaissance and the Reformation, along with the crisis of the 17th century and the revolutions of the 19th century, produced the economic basis for a new social culture in Western Europe — the culture of Capitalism. This breakdown of Feudalism led to social revolution — from Feudalism to Capitalism. This social revolution led to cultural revolution. The great art and the great culture of the Renaissance, in particular, was the result of the breakdown of Feudalism, the crisis of Feudalism, and the rise of Capitalism. The emergence of Capitalist culture emerged with the reality of the social revolution of Capitalism.1

The development of Capitalist culture reached its height during the bourgeois revolutions of the seventeenth, eighteenth, and nineteenth centuries. The English Revolution, the French Revolution, the American Revolution, and the Industrial Revolution, constituted the revolutionary height of Capitalist culture. This led to the greatest triumph of Capitalist culture and Capitalist art — in the period of the Industrial Revolution. Indeed, the height of Capitalist culture was probably in that period just before the outbreak of the First World War — as since then, since 1914, the culture of Capitalism has repeatedly fallen into barbarism. The really revolutionary forms of Capitalist society, during the bourgeois revolutions of the 1600s, 1700s, and 1800s, produced the mainly revolutionary forms of Capitalist culture. The ideas of Liberalism, Conservatism, Romanticism, the Enlightenment, and the long struggle to achieve the ideas of Socialism, emerged from these revolutionary developments. The revolutionary nature of the best forms of culture, under Capitalism, also highlights the possible fact that the best forms of culture emerge in periods of revolution and periods of revolutionary struggle. The development of Capitalist culture has declined, since the 1900s, because Capitalism itself has ceased to be a revolutionary force and has become a reactionary force. This is highlighted, in particular, by the reality of Capitalism as it exists today — in the form of Neo-Liberal Capitalism and Late-Stage Capitalism. Since the end of the Cold War, it is perhaps correct to say that the historical development of Capitalism, and the historical development of Capitalist culture, has reached its historical and political limit. The alternative, today, is either Socialism or Barbarism. The culture of Capitalism was once revolutionary and progressive, now it is simply reduced to reaction and to commercialism. The culture of Capitalism, today, is the culture of Late-Stage Capitalism.

The culture of Capitalism is the culture of accumulation. Capitalism, in the end, is a society based on accumulation. The culture of Capitalism, as it has historically evolved, and as it has politically evolved, is based on the culture of accumulation. Despite all the many ways in which a Capitalist culture can be created and maintained, across the long history of Capitalism, a key fundamental element, across the history of Capitalism, is the pursuit of profit and accumulation. Accumulation, in the end, is at the root of Capitalist culture. This is obvious in all Capitalist societies — from the 14th century to the present. Indeed, we can trace this vision of culture — from the origins of Capitalism to the present reality of Capitalism.

The culture of Capitalism is the culture of profit. Capitalism produces culture — but as a cultural system it only produces culture with the objective of making a profit. No real development of culture has occurred, for Capitalism, without the motivation of profit. Individual artists might create for art and for the sake of art, but for their backers, and for their patrons, the goal always remains the goal of profit. This can be seen as the reality of Capitalist culture since the beginning of Capitalism. In the Renaissance, the Italian City States supported art and culture — as part of the transition from Feudalism to Capitalism — but only as a means of generating wealth or showing off wealth. The power of Capitalist culture comes from this very basic economic goal — the goal of using art and culture to make profit at the expense of all other considerations.

The culture of Capitalism is the culture of growth. Capitalism only cares about culture if it can produce a profit. In many ways, this has led to the decline of art as a social force — with good art being ignored and bad art being promoted, based purely on what is not profitable and what is profitable. So long as Capitalism bases its structure of culture on this structure of profit it can never be argued that Capitalism cares about culture in artistic terms. For Capitalism, profit outweighs all other considerations — whether that is about society, culture, ecology, humanity, human well-being, culture, or art. This point is clear at any historical stage in the history of Capitalism. Indeed, Capitalism, like most class societies, has always sacrificed humanity for profit. In times of crisis this often leads to reaction, and even Fascism. Ever since the beginning of Capitalism, to the present, the economic structure of Capitalism cares only about the economic struggle for profit. This means that, in many ways, Capitalism is probably the most economically determinist mode of production in human history. It cares about society, culture, ecology, humanity, human well-being, culture, and art, in only economic terms.2 Capitalism cares about itself and its profits – not about humanity.

Capitalist culture, since the end of the Second World War, has become increasingly commercialised. The rise of mass culture and mass consumption are connected — especially in the Capitalist states of the West. By itself mass culture is excellent — as it leads to the rise of a genuinely popular culture, enjoyed by millions — but mass culture is also connected to the reality of culture under Capitalism. Mass culture might be excellent, but it can also be a culture which is crude, shallow, mass produced, and interested in ignoring the realities of human society.3

The culture of Capitalism has produced many great advances for human culture — from the Renaissance to the Industrial Revolution, from Romanticism to Popular Culture. Yet despite these advances the history of Capitalism, and the politics of Capitalism, have also produced awful forms of culture and awful forms of society. The reality of Fascism and Nazism, which were products of Capitalism, and the crisis of Capitalism, shows the reality that Capitalism can produce truly barbaric forms of society and culture. The development of human progress is not a linear development — as we now know given the reality of the First World War, the Second World War, the Cold War, and the results of Fascism and Nazism. Given these events, in the history of human society and human culture, we cannot assume that Capitalism will always produce a human society or a human culture. We must always remember, in the struggle for a better world, that the development of modern society can easily result in the reality of barbarism and the monstrosity of exploitation, oppression, sexism, racism, imperialism, genocide, and war. Capitalism might be able to produce wonders in terms of the development of human capacities — but it also has a dark side built into its development — because it is based, fundamentally, on exploitation and oppression. The historical development of human culture might have advanced forward due to the historical developments of Capitalism — but that history also shows the reality of barbarism. Human beings, if they are to have a better future, can never simply assume that Capitalism will produce the best of all worlds — as many Liberals and Conservatives assume. The history of Capitalism shows that Capitalism can be brutal — and is brutal. This is why the struggle for Socialism is so vital and so crucial. If we truly believe in the potential of humanity, in the potential of the values of the Enlightenment, we need to move beyond the limits of Capitalism and Capitalist society.

Capitalist culture has framed itself as the 'natural culture' of humanity. It sees itself as the inevitable, natural, society of humanity. This is ahistorical. Capitalism has not always existed. Capitalism is just a specific stage in human history — a mode of production. Capitalism has not always existed — and it will not always exist. Capitalism, since it has not always existed, cannot be the 'natural culture' of humanity for that historical reason. Humanity, and human culture, existed long before Capitalism. Hopefully, humanity, and human culture, will exist long after Capitalism is gone. This historical fact of human society and human culture undermines any argument suggesting that Capitalism is the 'natural' basis of human culture. Capitalism is a recent development in human history. Even the longest historical argument for Capitalism only goes back to the 1400s or the 1500s — with the beginning of the crisis of Feudalism in the 14th century. The culture of Capitalism is historical. The culture of Capitalism is so historical that it can be argued that the culture of Capitalism is not the default culture of human beings — or the ideal basis for human beings. Hopefully, a better society and a better culture can be created — a Socialist society, a Socialist culture.

The concrete reality of Capitalist culture is political. The culture of Capitalism cannot escape the fact that it is part of Capitalism. Only the delusional person, or a capitalist, would claim that the ideas of culture, today, are not part of Capitalism. The ruling ideas, after all, are the ideas of the ruling system. The reality of our society, as a Capitalist society, means that the ruling ideas of today are Capitalist ideas.4

It is impossible to separate culture from society. Culture emerges from society. Culture emerges from the social base of society. Culture is part of the social superstructure of society. This fact, of history, means that culture, under Capitalism, is an expression of Capitalism. Capitalist culture is part of the social superstructure of Capitalism.

The theory of Historical Materialism explains the real connection between culture and society. Society produces culture by creating culture as part of the social superstructure of society. Capitalist society creates Capitalist culture — by creating culture as part of the superstructure of Capitalist society. This process is a historical process, a political process, a cultural process, and a social process. The history of Capitalist culture is, then, part of the history of Capitalist society.

We live in a class society which has produced a particular form of class culture. This culture, as part of society, has emerged due to the history and politics of human society — since the emergence of the human species and humanity. In our times, today, our culture is part of Capitalist society. Marx, in his effective study of human society, understood that culture is reflective of wider human society. Culture changes because human society changes. If we wish to achieve a better form of culture, we must change society. For Marx this shows the importance of social revolution in the development of society and the development of culture. For Marx, we must go beyond class society and beyond class culture if we really wish to see the development of culture. We must achieve Socialism – if we want a free society.

While Capitalist culture remains the dominant form of culture in the world, today, its decline is obvious — and has been obvious since the realities of the First World War, the Second World War, the Cold War, and the rise of Neo-Liberalism. Capitalism, in historical and political terms, has created a powerful culture, but this powerful culture cannot overcome the inherent problems and contradictions of Capitalism itself. As with all cultures, throughout history, the culture of Capitalism cannot overcome the real problems and contradictions of its own society. The problems of Capitalism, itself, in historical, economic, political, and cultural terms, generates the problems of Capitalist culture. A culture with a declining society is a culture which will suffer decline in the long run — no matter how much it generates or how much it dominates existing society. The culture of Capitalism, in the long run, has no future. While Capitalism itself might go on for a long period of time, into the future, it will, inevitably, be replaced by a different society — and a different mode of production. The culture of Capitalism is a historical culture — it had an origin, and it will have an end. We might not live to see the end of Capitalism and Capitalist culture, but it will end in the long run — given enough history, given enough politics, and given enough social development. The revolutions of history and the revolutions of politics, in the foreseeable future of the human race, will eventually lead to a new society and a new culture. That new society and that new culture will either be Socialism, or it will be Barbarism. The struggle of today, for today, is the struggle to ensure that the culture and the society of the future is Socialism. In social terms the future of Capitalism is a simple choice for humanity — either we will achieve Socialism, or we shall see the end of human culture.

Capitalism is not the eternal basis for human society or human culture. Since Capitalism has not existed for all of human history there is always a basis for a different form of human society — namely Socialism. For Marx, the real basis of human culture is the ability of human beings to create themselves and their societies — through labour. This means that the history and politics of Capitalism, and Capitalist culture, need to be seen in the context of human history as a whole. Capitalism, and Capitalist culture, are simply periods in human history — modes of production. In the end, Capitalism will be replaced by something else, hopefully Socialism, because human beings continue to create, re-create, reproduce, and labour. Our capacity as a species, for labour and for creation, is the real material basis for our advances as a species. Marx, himself, outlined this reality in his theory of Historical Materialism. Marx clearly outlined this in his book 'The German Ideology' (1846):

> The first premise of all human history is, of course, the existence of living human individuals. Thus, the first fact to be established is the physical organisation of these individuals and their consequent relation to the rest of nature. ... Men can be distinguished from animals by consciousness, by religion or anything else you like. They themselves begin to distinguish themselves from animals as soon as they begin to produce their means of subsistence, a step which is conditioned by their physical organisation. By producing their means of subsistence men are indirectly producing their actual material life.5

Human beings, because of labour and because of society, are capable of creating a free culture. If we wish to have a truly free culture we must, first, build a free society. It is only when we have built a free society, a Socialist society, that we can really seek to build a free culture. It is on this basis that we might build a culture based on the free development of each and the free development of all.6

Capitalist society proclaims itself to be a free society — and yet it is built on top of a reality of exploitation and oppression. Indeed, the reality of Capitalist culture, for all its achievements and all its wonders, is that it remains limited by its economic base — a class society of exploitation and oppression. All of the good of Capitalist culture is stained with the reality of the history and the politics which had to be generated, in blood, in suffering and in revolution, to generate Capitalism itself. Capitalist society might be better than Feudal society – but it is still Capitalism.

Capitalism is not a neutral system. It is a system of exploitation and oppression. This reality of exploitation and oppression is part of the reality of Capitalist culture.

We can only understand Capitalist culture when we understand that its roots lie in Capitalism itself. While Capitalist culture might profess its independence from society, such as in the idea of 'art for art's sake', Capitalist culture is still connected to Capitalism. This means that it cannot escape from the history and politics of Capitalism. The rise and fall of Capitalist culture, in the end, is linked, completely, to Capitalism. With the fall of Capitalism, we shall see the fall of Capitalist culture.

Notes

1. K. Marx and F. Engels, The Communist Manifesto, (1848)
2. K. Marx and F. Engels, The Communist Manifesto, (1848)
3. M. Horkheimer and T. Adorno, Dialectic of Enlightenment, (1947)
4. K. Marx and F. Engels, The Communist Manifesto, (1848)
5. K. Marx, The German Ideology, (1845)
6. K. Marx and F. Engels, The Communist Manifesto, (1848)

(2016)

CHAPTER VI

CAPITALIST CULTURE – PROBLEMS OF CAPITALIST CULTURE

This short essay is a study of the problems of Capitalist culture. Culture is in crisis today. Capitalism is in crisis today. Capitalism, today, is suffering a major crisis – an economic crisis, a political crisis, a social crisis, and a cultural crisis. Capitalism is incapable of solving those problems – both in the short term and in the long term. It is important, from the perspective of the Left, to outline the problems of Capitalism – including the culture of Capitalism and the cultural ideas of Capitalism. Capitalism, today, clearly cannot solve its problems – including its cultural problems. All the contemporary problems of Capitalism point to problems with its culture. This brief essay is a brief outline of the key problems surrounding the problems of Capitalist culture and the problems of culture under Capitalism.

Capitalist society and Capitalist culture produced many advances. Capitalist society and Capitalist culture have produced a great deal of positives for humanity and for human society. The advances of the last three centuries show that Capitalism was once a revolutionary force and a radical force – one which achieved positive change for humanity. Humanity owes Capitalism a great deal – as Marx himself said when he described Capitalism as a revolutionary force.1 Capitalism, today, is no longer a revolutionary force.2 Capitalism, today, is no longer a revolutionary force for culture.3

Capitalism has reached a serious point of crisis. This includes the culture of Capitalism. Given the problems of Capitalism, today, it is clear that this aspect of Capitalism is over. Capitalism is no longer a revolutionary or radical force.

Capitalism has reached a point of cultural crisis. This crisis is obvious if we look at the reality of the culture of Capitalism in all its forms. Capitalism, and its culture, is slowly slipping away into the dust-pin of History – just like all previous societies and all previous cultures. Humanity will need to find a different solution to the problems of Capitalism – one outside of Capitalism itself.

Capitalism has reached a point of social crisis. This crisis is obvious in the reality of Capitalist society. Capitalist society has conquered the world – and yet it is incapable of solving the problems which confront it and its society.

Capitalist culture prides itself in believing it is the ultimate form of culture. This is because of the fact that Capitalism, at this point in history, has conquered most of the world and most places in the world. Most forms of culture, today, are either Capitalist culture or expressions of Capitalist culture. Despite this it is clear that Capitalist culture, culture under Capitalism is undergoing its decline and its fall. The nature of this decline is currently shaping the nature of culture under Capitalism. The nature of this decline is also shaping the type of culture which is produced under Capitalism. Capitalist culture, today, might be triumphant, but it is obvious that it cannot develop any further. Having conquered the globe for its commodities and its ideas, Capitalism now has no further way to expand or develop itself. Cultures which cannot expand tend to die. Cultures which cannot develop tend to die. Cultures which repress, rather than liberate, tend to die. Cultures which exploit, rather than liberate, tend to die. Capitalist culture, today, shows signs of all of these problems. The fact that Capitalist culture is based on profit, and not on culture, is another problem. All of this means that while Capitalism can continue to produce culture, and profit from culture, it can no longer develop itself or Human culture. The inability of Capitalism to overcome its systemic problems will, inevitably, lead to a decline of culture under Capitalism. The inability of Capitalism to develop itself will be part of the reason why Capitalism will fail in the end – and be replaced by Socialism. Marx, himself, understood this problem for culture under Capitalism. This means that culture, under Capitalism, is ultimately a dying culture.

The world is now a single economic unit. Capitalism has reached every part of the globe at this point in history. This means that Capitalism has created a global society and a global culture. This also means that the problems of Capitalism and the problems of Capitalist culture are now universal. These problems exist everywhere, and they are being challenged everywhere – by the ideas of Socialism and by the struggle for Socialism.

Capitalist culture has become a worldwide culture. It has exported itself – via art, economics, politics, and society – to every corner of the globe and to every part of the planet. This makes the culture of Capitalism a powerful social force. This also means that Capitalism, in its constant revolutions and its constant developments, has created the basis for a better society and a better culture – for Socialism and for a Socialist culture. The working class, today, is bigger than at any other time in world history. The working class, today, is also developing its own culture and its own ideas about culture. This means that just as Capitalism has triumphed in terms of creating an international world and an international culture it has also generated the basis for its overthrow by the working class. Capitalism, and its culture, have triumphed – but they have also generated the struggles by which they will be overthrown and replaced by a different society – by Socialism and by a Socialist society.

The crisis in Capitalism is a worldwide crisis. The crisis in Capitalist culture is a worldwide crisis. Capitalism is undermining culture because it places profit over art as the basis for culture and for cultural development. If one asks a Capitalist what their relationship with art is, they will tell you that their relationship with art is to make money and profit from art. This means that Capitalism, in the end, is a destructive force for art. Capitalism only cares for art and culture in that it can sell and profit from it. This, in the short term, is not a major concern for Capitalist society and for Capitalist culture, but it means, in the long run, that Capitalism will produce a declining culture – because it is incapable of putting the greater good and the greater development of art and culture ahead of profit and accumulation. The death of art and culture under Capitalism is the result of Capitalism placing profit and the profit motive ahead of everything else in the development of art and culture. This mentality signals the destruction of art. This mentality signals the destruction of culture. This mentality also means that Capitalism cannot maintain culture in the long run. In the long run Capitalist culture must be replaced by something else. Capitalist culture must be replaced by Socialism.

Capitalism is in despair over the crisis of its culture. Many of the biggest supporters of Capitalism, today, despair over the idea that Capitalism and its culture cannot solve the problems which surround them. Indeed, this has become a major part of the cultural discussion of the Right and the Far-Right in many parts of Capitalist politics and Capitalist culture. The inability of Capitalism to solve its economic problems and its social problems often means that Capitalism blames its own problems on cultural problems – and on cultural decline. The reality, however, is that the cultural problems of Capitalism are the result of the economic problems and the social problems of Capitalism. Those Capitalists who criticise the cultural decline of Capitalist society have reversed the reality of the crisis. In reality the root of the crisis in culture lies in the reality of the crisis of Capitalism itself. The only way to solve the crisis of the culture of Capitalism is to overcome Capitalism – and to replace it with something else. Capitalism, in the end, must be overcome and overthrown. Capitalism, and its culture, must be overthrown by Socialism.

If defenders of culture truly wish to solve the problems of culture they will need to break with Capitalism. Capitalism will continue to undermine culture until it is overthrown. The problems of Capitalism and its culture cannot be solved by changes in culture – they can only be solved by social conflict, social struggle, and by the triumph of Socialism.

If defenders of Capitalism truly wish to understand the problems of Capitalist culture, they will need to dig deeper than simply the modern problems of Capitalist culture. They will need to engage with the real social reality of Capitalism – its exploitation, its oppression, and its misery. Of course, such defenders of Capitalism will never do this. They will never do this because that would mean they would have to be honest about the reality of Capitalism. The reality of Capitalism is simply the social reality of exploitation and oppression. By engaging with the reality of Capitalism, specifically its problems and its exploitation, this fundamentally weakens Capitalism itself, and makes the argument for Socialism.

We can now outline the key problems of Capitalist culture. The key problems of Capitalist culture are economic, social, political, and cultural.

The economic problems of Capitalist culture are that Capitalist culture is increasingly becoming monopolised and incapable of economic progress. The cost of Capitalist culture is slowly undermining it at the economic level.

The social problems of Capitalist culture are that Capitalist culture is increasingly unable to maintain its hegemony over modern society. Modern society is increasingly becoming tired and frustrated by the limits of Capitalist culture and the alienation of Capitalist culture.

The political problems of Capitalist culture are that Capitalist culture is shifting further and further to the Right. This means that it will, eventually, alienate the working class. This means that the culture of Capitalism will become increasingly desperate and barbaric.

The cultural problems of Capitalist culture are that Capitalist culture is increasingly becoming monopolised in terms of cultural ideas. This means that Capitalist culture is rapidly running out of new ideas and new developments.

We can now turn to how the problems of Capitalist culture relate to the problems of Capitalism, and Capitalist Hegemony, today. These problems are crucial to understand in order to understand Capitalism and to overcome Capitalism – to understand Capitalism in order to replace it with Socialism.

Capitalist culture, Capitalist society, and Capitalist economics are the basis of Capitalist Hegemony. Hegemony is the domination of society by a ruling class. Hegemony, specifically, is how a ruling class dominates the economics, society, politics, and culture of a society. Capitalist Hegemony, specifically, is a hegemony which is dominated by the Capitalist class. If the hegemony of Capitalism is to be broken, and replaced by Socialism, this will require a Socialist critique of both culture and economics under Capitalism, in order to develop a Socialist Hegemony – a hegemony of the working class. This is the basis of the ideas of Gramsci regarding culture and cultural hegemony – specifically that the working class must overcome the cultural hegemony of Capitalism, alongside the economic, social, and political hegemony of Capitalism, in order to build Socialism. Gramsci, like Marx, believed that in order for Socialism to be built the working class must challenge the hegemony of Capitalism and the Capitalist class, by creating its own economic, political, and social hegemony. Gramsci developed his ideas in order to reinforce the struggle for Socialism. When the culture of Capitalism is understood the struggle for Socialism is possible. The struggle for Socialism is the answer to the problems of Capitalist culture.

If we want to understand the problems of Capitalism today, we must understand the problems of Capitalist culture. We need to understand the economic, political, historical, and social problems of Capitalism – but also the cultural problems of Capitalism. If we are to ever understand Capitalism, we must understand all parts of Capitalism – including the culture which supports it. This will allow us to develop the politics and economics needed in order to overcome Capitalism, and to replace it with Socialism. This was the basis of Gramsci's idea of Hegemony and Cultural Hegemony. Capitalist Hegemony is the economic, political, and cultural basis of

Capitalist power. This form of hegemony allows Capitalism to dominate modern society. If we can understand the Cultural hegemony of Capitalism, we will have the ability to overcome Capitalism – and the ability to replace it with Socialism.

For Marxists it is vital to understand the problems of Capitalist culture. For Marxists it is vital to solve the problems of culture under Capitalism. This is because it is vital to develop an alternative – both to Capitalism and to Capitalist culture. It is vital to develop Socialism and to develop a Socialist culture. Socialist culture, in the end, must overcome Capitalist culture.

Socialism is better than Capitalism. This is not simply an ideological statement – it is a statement of fact. This can be shown in economic terms, political terms, social terms, and historical terms. This can also be shown in cultural terms. Socialism can develop human culture better than Capitalism because Socialism places humanity before profit, and because Socialism places culture before profit. The power of Socialist culture is both its co-operative development and its human development. Socialist culture, in the end, will overcome Capitalist culture. The power of the working class, to create its own culture, historically and politically, also shows the power of Socialism – and its superiority over Capitalism.

The hegemony of Capitalism relies on Capitalist culture. The weakening of Capitalist culture reinforces the weakening of Capitalism itself. The fact that Capitalist culture and Capitalist society are in decline, today, suggests that Capitalism cannot maintain the hegemony of its culture or the hegemony of its own economics and politics. Into this situation the need for an alternative culture and an alternative society becomes more pressing. The reality of the crisis of Capitalism is the basis to start constructing an alternative to Capitalism and a replacement to Capitalism. This replacement to Capitalism, in social terms, in political terms, in economic terms, in cultural terms, can only be Socialism. Socialism is the only economic system and the only political system which can overcome Capitalism today – due to its economic basis and its political basis in the majority of the population and in the majority of the world. The struggle for a Socialist culture is the struggle both to overcome Capitalism and to develop a Socialist society. Socialism can replace the culture of Capitalism because it is objectively a more humane and more human culture. Capitalism, with its basis on exploitation and oppression, cannot produce a better culture than Socialism. Socialism, with its basis in equality and co-operation, can produce a better culture than Capitalism. The conflict between Capitalism and Socialism is a conflict which only highlights the superiority of Socialism as the basis for a real culture and for a real humanity. Capitalism might be able to hold back the coming revolution of Socialism, but it cannot hold this revolution back forever. Sooner or later the triumph of Socialism will overcome the problems of Capitalism. Capitalism can resist this triumph – in the reality of class struggle and class conflict – but it cannot hold this triumph back forever. The very nature of the progression of humanity, culture, society, and economics points the way for the victory of Socialism. The development of Capitalism and Capitalist culture points the way to the victory of Socialism and the victory of Socialist culture.

The history of the culture of Capitalism is the history of Capitalism exploiting culture. The history of the culture of Capitalism also shows that it cannot reform itself beyond a certain limit. The limits of Capitalist culture might reform themselves – but they cannot prevent the crisis of Capitalism or the crisis of Capitalist culture.

Culture will not die because of Capitalism. As long as humanity exists there will always be some development of culture. What Capitalism might do, however, is limit the development of culture to such an extent that culture might die anyway. Capitalism, with its interests in profits, is not interested in culture. This means that the interests of Capitalism and the interests of culture are opposing interests.

We need to find a way to solve the problems of culture – by seeking out a better form of culture. We need to find a way to revitalise culture and a way to revolutionise culture. Capitalist culture, because of its interests, cannot solve the problems of culture. Only Social Revolution can solve the problems of culture. Only Socialist Revolution can solve the problems of culture.

Capitalism is not capable of solving the problems of Capitalism. Capitalism is not capable of solving the economic problems of Capitalism. Capitalism is not capable of solving the cultural problems of Capitalism. This reality means, in the long run, that Capitalism is doomed – and will be replaced by a different mode of production – by Socialism. This reality should be clear to anyone who truthfully engages with the reality of Capitalism as both a social system and as a cultural system. Capitalism had its beginning. Capitalism will have its end. Capitalist culture had its beginning. Capitalist culture will have its end. Capitalism is not interested in solving its problems. Indeed, Capitalism has never sought to solve its problems – instead, it merely moves its problems around society and ignores them. This results in the economic crises of Capitalism – but also in the social crises and cultural crises of Capitalism. Since Capitalism is incapable of solving its economic crises, it is impossible for Capitalism to solve its social crises or its cultural crises. This inability of Capitalism to come to terms with its social problems and cultural problems is another reason why Capitalism, like all class societies, will eventually be overcome by its problems. Defenders of Capitalism might seek to reform the system – here and there – in order to save it – but the political reality of Capitalism means that its destruction is inevitable. Capitalism will continue to expand itself, its industry, and the working class. This expansion will, in the end, generate the forces capable of overcoming Capitalism – namely the working class and working-class revolution. The working class will not only make revolution, but they will make culture – a better culture. If there is any hope for culture and for society, then it lies with the working class.

Humanity is based on culture. Humanity and Humanism is based on culture. Without culture and without social development, humanity risks regressing to an earlier state – a worse state, a barbaric state. In those circumstances the problems of Capitalist culture become more obvious. These problems need to be overcome – with a better society and with a better culture. Socialism can build such a better culture.

The crisis of Capitalist culture will be different in different countries. Indeed, in several countries the crisis might even destroy the basic assumptions of their culture – such as the culture of the United States. A better culture needs to replace Capitalism and Capitalist culture. What has to be struggled for, here and now, is a better culture – a culture based on social progress, social liberation, and social equality. Only Socialism can both free culture and develop culture. Only Socialism can overcome the problems of Capitalist culture.

Culture, today, requires revolution. The stagnation of Capitalist society has caused a stagnation in the development of culture. The political struggle for a better culture is part of any social struggle for a better society. Socialism is the basis of this social struggle – for a better culture.4

If we believe in a truly human culture, then the culture of Capitalism has to be defeated. Capitalism cannot build a human culture or a humane culture. The only way to build a human culture or a humane culture is through Socialism.5

The problems of Capitalist culture ultimately undermine Capitalism. The struggle to understand the culture of Capitalism helps to develop the struggle for Socialism. Socialism can replace Capitalism. Socialism will replace Capitalism.6

The problems of Capitalist culture are the problems of Capitalism. The solutions of Socialist culture are the solutions of Socialism. Humanity will have to choose between them – between Barbarism and Socialism.

Notes

1. K. Marx and F. Engels, The Communist Manifesto, (1848)
2. K. Marx and F. Engels, The Communist Manifesto, (1848)
3. M. Horkheimer and T. Adorno, Dialectic of Enlightenment, (1947)
4. R. Williams, The Long Revolution, (1961)
5. R. Williams, The Long Revolution, (1961)
6. K. Marx and F. Engels, The Communist Manifesto, (1848)

(2016)

CHAPTER VII

STAGES OF CAPITALISM

This short essay is a study of the stages of Capitalism. Capitalism has gone through a number of historical periods — since its emergence out of Feudalism and out of the transition from Feudalism. These stages form a key part of the history and development of Capitalism, as an economic, social, political, and intellectual reality of human history and human society. In order to fully understand the development of Capitalism we must understand the stages of Capitalism.1 Capitalism was a revolutionary and progressive development in human history — by producing the economic, social, political, and human development needed for Socialism.

We can outline the stages of Capitalism. These stages of Capitalism form the basis by which Capitalism has emerged since the crisis of Feudalism and since the transition from Feudalism to Capitalism (1450-1850). These stages are: Primitive Accumulation (1450-1750), Bourgeois Revolution (1600-1848), Industrial Revolution (1750-1850), Industrial Capitalism (1850-present), Imperialism (1880-present), and Neo-Liberalism (1980-present). In order to really understand Capitalism, we must understand its development. By understanding the development of Capitalism, we might be in a better position to understand the struggle for Socialism.2

We can outline the stages of the development of Capitalism:

Stage I — Primitive Accumulation. Primitive Accumulation was the process of the early development of Capitalism. Primitive Accumulation was the process of the development of the first forms of Capital accumulation in the world. This process emerged out of the crisis of Feudalism (the 14th century), the rise of Agrarian Capitalism, the conquest of the New World, the scientific revolution, the process of enclosure, the process of slavery and the Atlantic slave trade, and the process of early colonialism. These developments, taken together, formed the early history of Capitalism — as it struggled to emerge out of Feudalism in Europe. In economic terms and social terms, Primitive Accumulation constituted the early years of Capitalist development — providing the economic and social basis for Industrial Capitalism. The first Capitalist Societies emerged between 1400 and 1750 — namely in England, France, the Dutch Republic, and the Italian City States. These early Capitalist societies went on to form the basis for much subsequent Capitalist development. Primitive Accumulation was a long process, one which developed over multiple centuries, but it effectively formed the transition from Feudalism to Capitalism, the rise of Capitalism, and the rise of Industrial Capitalism. Primitive Accumulation, in economic terms, social terms, and historical terms, was the birth of Capitalism.

Stage II — Bourgeois Revolution. Bourgeois revolution was the process of the development of Capitalism via political revolution and social revolution. In the 1600s, 1700s, and 1800s, there were a series of revolutions which established the development of Capitalism in political terms. A bourgeois revolution is any revolution led by a capitalist class which furthers the economic, political, and social development of Capitalism. Most of these revolutions took place during the 19th century — during the process of the Industrial Revolution. Bourgeois revolution can be considered part of the process of democratic revolution — establishing bourgeois democracy. These revolutions led to the final fall of Feudalism and the final rise of Capitalism. The best known of these revolutions were: the English Revolution of 1640, the Glorious Revolution of 1688, the Dutch Revolt, the American Revolution of 1776, the French Revolution of 1789, the Latin American Wars of Independence, the Revolutions of 1848, German unification, Italian unification, the Meiji Restoration, and the American Civil War. These revolutions allowed Capitalism to become a political force — replacing Feudalism as a political force. These revolutions constituted the first modern revolutions in world history and world politics — allowing Capitalism to firmly establish itself as a modern political system. These revolutions completed the economic and political transition from Feudalism to Capitalism, in several countries, and allowed the political basis for the Industrial Revolution of the 19th century.

Stage III — Industrial Revolution. The Industrial Revolution was the process of transforming Feudalism, and earlier periods of Capitalism, into Industrial Capitalism. The Industrial Revolution was the greatest economic and social revolution ever unleashed by Capitalism. The Industrial Revolution began in Britain — transforming that country into the 'Workshop of the World' for most of the 19th century. The Industrial Revolution was the greatest social revolution of the 19th century — as it created Industrial

Capitalism in Great Britain, France, Germany, the United States, and other parts of Europe. This revolution spread across Europe and had reached many parts of the world by the end of the 19th century. The greatest political revolution unleashed by the Industrial Revolution was the great age of revolution between 1789 and 1848, from the French Revolution of 1789 to the Revolutions of 1848. These revolutions unleashed the full development of bourgeois society and the full development of Capitalist society. The Industrial Revolution also created new classes — specifically the class of industrial capitalists and the class of industrial workers. The Industrial Revolution, as a social revolution, created the modern capitalist class and the modern working class. The Industrial Revolution, in economic terms, created the basis for much of Capitalist society as we currently understand it. The Industrial Revolution, in social terms, created the basis for the development of much of the modern world.

Stage IV — Industrial Capitalism. Industrial Capitalism has been the dominant form of Capitalism since 1850. Since the emergence of Industrial Capitalism, we have lived in an industrial world. This industrial world has led to the great expansion in economic development which we have seen since the 1750s and since the 1850s. This level of industrial development remains the greatest victory of Capitalist society — despite its exploitation, its oppression, and its Imperialism. It is also via the process of Industrial Capitalism that the possibility for Socialism emerges — as Capitalism creates both the level of development needed for Socialism, and the working class needed for Socialism. In political terms Industrial Capitalism, despite de-industrialisation, still remains the key basis of most Capitalist states and most Capitalist societies. Industrial Capitalism, today, has spread to most societies and most parts of the globe — since the 19th century, since the 20th century, and since the 21st century. The process of Capitalist development and the process of Capitalist society has given rise to the possibility for Socialism. We live in a world, today, which is slowly beginning the process towards the transition towards Socialism. Either humanity will shift towards Socialism, in the coming century, or humanity will be faced with the prospect of barbarism. Capitalism, today, has reached its highest stage of social development, economic development, and political development. Capitalism must be replaced by Socialism.

Stage V — Imperialism. Imperialism is the highest stage of Capitalism. Imperialism, in the modern world, is the division of the world for Capitalist exploitation. We currently live in the Imperialist stage of Capitalism. This process of Capitalism emerged in the late 19th century, with the expansion of Empires and the expansion of the world market. Lenin's theory of Imperialism remains vital for understanding Imperialism — both in the early 20th century and today. Imperialism is the expansion of Capitalism to all parts of the world. Imperialism, as a stage of Capitalism, occurs when Capitalism reaches the highest forms of Capitalist production. Imperialism is (1) the concentration of production and capital reaching a certain level in the history of Capitalism, (2) Industrial Capitalism being replaced by Finance Capitalism, (3) the export of capital, (4) the formation of monopoly Capitalism, and (5) the division of the world among the biggest Capitalist powers. Imperialism has led to the division of the world into a series of Capitalist markets. Lenin's theory of Imperialism helps to explain the subsequent development of Capitalism since the 1880s — from the 1880s to today. In our current times, of Neo-Liberalism, we still live in the Imperialist stage of Capitalism, but in a slightly different form. Imperialism remains the most dangerous form of Capitalism — as competition between the Capitalist Powers led, both directly and indirectly, to the World Wars, especially the First World War of 1914-1918.

Stage VI — Neo-Liberalism. Neo-Liberalism has been the form of Capitalism which has dominated since the 1970s and since the 1980s. In economic terms, Neo-Liberalism has seen a major restructuring of Capitalism, based on economic liberalisation, political liberalisation, privatisation, the restructuring of Capitalist industry and Capitalist society, free markets, and the rapid expansion of Capitalism itself. In political terms, Neo-Liberalism has dominated the world since the end of the Cold War and since the collapse of the Soviet Union in 1991. Neo-Liberalism, specifically, was the means of saving Capitalism from the crisis of the 1970s, and from the breakdown of the post-war order in the 1970s. Neo-Liberalism has dominated the political-economy of most Capitalist societies since the 1980s, especially in the United States and the United Kingdom. Neo-Liberalism, in effective terms, is how most Capitalist states and Capitalist societies operate today. Neo-Liberalism has been in crisis since 2007/2008, since the great financial crisis of 2007/2008. The future economic development of Neo-Liberalism is impossible to predict. We cannot know what direction Neo-Liberalism will take Capitalism in the coming decades. Hopefully, the future will be a Socialist future — a future based on overcoming Capitalism and Neo-Liberalism. Today we live in a period of major Capitalist crisis — a crisis brought about by the crisis of Capitalism itself, and by the crisis of Neo-Liberalism. The only way to end the crisis of Neo-Liberalism is to end the crisis of Capitalism itself – by achieving Socialism.

Notes

1. K. Marx, Capital Vol. I, (1867)
2. V.I. Lenin, Imperialism, (1917)

(2014)

CHAPTER VIII

STAGES OF CAPITALIST CULTURE

This short essay is a study of the stages of Capitalist culture. In order to fully understand the development of Capitalism and the culture of Capitalism we must understand the historical development of Capitalism since the 1500s. Capitalism has gone through a series of stages and a series of developments. These have shaped the development of Capitalism — but also the development of Capitalist culture.1

We can outline the stages of Capitalist culture. Capitalism has gone through the following, main, stages of development: Primitive Accumulation (1450-1750), Bourgeois Revolution (1600-1848), Industrial Revolution (1750-1850), Industrial Capitalism (1850-present), Imperialism (1880-present), and Neo-Liberalism (1980-present). These stages of Capitalism and Capitalist development have shaped the development of Capitalist culture. These stages also represent the stages of Capitalist culture.2

We can outline the stages of the development of Capitalist culture:

Stage I: Primitive Accumulation. Primitive Accumulation provided the first economic basis for Capitalist culture. This period dominated Capitalist development between 1450 and 1750. This development of Capitalist culture occurred, mainly, in Western Europe — as Capitalism emerged and Feudalism declined. The process of Primitive Accumulation produced the first major ideas for Capitalist culture — grounding them in the economic development of the 1400s, 1500s, 1600s, and 1700s. The development of culture, in this period, was shaped by the rise of the first Capitalist societies — specifically England, France, the Dutch Republic, and the Italian City States. The culture of the Renaissance was the first major victory of Capitalism and Capitalist culture. These victories, also, signalled the last stand of Feudal art and Feudal culture, in Europe, prior to the final development of Capitalism. Art and culture, under Primitive Accumulation, was the art and culture of the first major period of the transition from Feudalism to Capitalism (1450-1850). The best examples of Capitalist culture, in this period, were the high culture of the Renaissance, Mannerism, Baroque, Rococo, early Neoclassicism, early Romanticism, early modern English literature, early modern French literature, Italian art, and the development of bourgeois ideas about culture, art, literature, and architecture.

Stage II — Bourgeois Revolution. Bourgeois revolutions are social revolutions which further the development of Capitalism, and which provide a serious social basis for Capitalist culture. This period of revolution, over centuries, produced much of the basis for bourgeois culture — in several places and in several societies. The bourgeois revolutions of the 17th century, the 18th century, and the 19th century, produced a process of social revolution and cultural revolution for bourgeois society, bourgeois culture, bourgeois ideas, and bourgeois art. Each major bourgeois revolution produced a further basis to Capitalist culture and Capitalist art. The English Revolution produced the cultural ideas of Puritanism, and part of the Protestant work ethic. The American Revolution produced the basis of American bourgeois culture. The French Revolution furthered the development of Romanticism and the ideas of the Enlightenment. The Revolutions of 1848 helped to spread new bourgeois ideas about art, culture, and society, across Europe and the world. Each major bourgeois revolution led as much to the development of Capitalist culture as to the development of Capitalism itself. Bourgeois revolution is an economic, social, political, intellectual, and scientific revolution — but it is also a cultural revolution. The best examples of Capitalist culture, in this period, were: late Romanticism, late Neoclassicism, Realism, Impressionism, British literature, French literature, American literature, Japanese literature (Meiji period), German literature (Second Reich), and the development of modern bourgeois revolutionary ideas about the enlightenment, rationality, liberty, equality, and fraternity.

Stage III — Industrial Revolution. Industrial Revolution provided the industrial basis for Capitalist culture. The Industrial Revolution allowed culture to be mass produced in an unheard-of way in human history — when compared to previous forms of culture. The Industrial Revolution, in terms of culture, saw the rapid expansion of the ability to produce culture — by revolutionising the means of production and the social relations of production. The Industrial Revolution was the most important development of culture since the emergence of Feudalism and the rise of the Renaissance, as it provided the economic basis for the creation of new forms of culture — culture which stood outside the limits of ancient society, feudal society, and early Capitalist society. The revolution in industry in the 1800s produced a revolution in art, culture, literature, and architecture. The Industrial Revolution also saw the emergence of the working class, as a social force and as a political force. The emergence of the working class led to the rise of working-class culture — and the development of a Socialist culture. The Industrial Revolution, from 1750-1850, created the basis for the first universal forms of culture — culture which was universal and overcame the limits of space, time, nationality, religion, and other forms of social division. This period of cultural development was difficult — due to the social reality of the Industrial Revolution — but it also led to greater advances in the fields of culture. The best examples of Capitalist culture, in this period, were: Romanticism, Neoclassicism, Impressionism, and Realism. There were further advances in British literature, French literature, American literature, Japanese literature (Meiji period), and German literature during this period.

Stage IV — Industrial Capitalism. Industrial Capitalism has been the dominant form of Capitalism since 1850 — and it has shaped the development of Capitalist culture. The overall process of culture, under Industrial Capitalism, has been the rapid development of the means of producing culture, and the rapid development of the means of developing culture. Capitalist culture, since the rise of Industrial Capitalism, has been shaped by the reality of mass production and mechanical production. Industrial Capitalism has also led, specifically, to the development of a type of Capitalist culture which has dominated the world since the 1950s — specifically mass production, mass consumerism, mass consumption, and the shaping of art and culture for the process of profit and accumulation. We, today, still live in an industrial Capitalist world, despite the rise of Neo-Liberalism and despite the rise of Late-Capitalist economics. Specifically, we live in an era of Late-Capitalism. The fundamental basis of Capitalism, today, still remains shaped by the process of industrial production and industrial accumulation — which has also shaped the production and consumption of culture in modern society. The best examples of culture, from this period, are: Modern Art, Contemporary Art, the Pre-Raphaelites, Surrealism, Social Realism, and Abstract Expressionism. In terms of writing this period of Capitalism saw the height of classic bourgeois literature, particularly in Britain, France, Germany, the United States, Russia, China, and Japan. Since the 1950s and the 1960s, since the end of Empires, we have also seen the expansion of new forms of culture and art — in Latin America, in Africa, and in Asia. This period of Industrial Capitalism also saw the development of a working-class culture — and the potential for a Socialist culture.

Stage V — Imperialism. Imperialism, as the highest stage of Capitalism, led to a serious decline in the advances of Capitalist culture. Imperialism, as a stage of Capitalism, emerged in the 1880s and led to a major shift in the direction and focus of Capitalist culture — particularly in the arts. Imperialism also led to a significant decline in Capitalist culture after 1914 — after the rise of the modern Empires, modern colonialism, and the brutality of the World Wars. Capitalist culture, as a unified culture, has been in decline since 1914 — since the outbreak of the First World War. This decline was due to the fact that Imperialism, as a process of Capitalism, led to barbarism, war, and genocide, in the process of the development of Capitalism. The high point of bourgeois culture, between 1789 and 1914, came crashing down in the reality of the First World War, the Second World War, and the Cold War. The political reality of Imperialism, of dividing up the world into a series of Capitalist markets, led to the degeneration of bourgeois culture as a social force. Capitalism, and Capitalist culture, still exists today, despite the barbarism of Imperialism, but its cultural force is completely undermined by the reality of Imperialism. Despite Imperialism there have been some serious developments in culture, under Capitalism, since the 1880s. In terms of culture the age of Imperialism has led to some serious artistic advances, particularly Post-impressionism, Neo-impressionism, Expressionism, Art Nouveau, Art Deco, Cubism, and Modern Art. The reality of Imperialism, from the 1880s, to today, has also led to the rise of art and culture opposed to both Capitalism and Imperialism — in the form of Socialist art and Socialist culture. Capitalist culture, under Imperialism, is the culture of Barbarism.

Stage VI — Neo-Liberalism. Neo-Liberalism, as the current form of Capitalism, has led to an expansion of culture — but it has also led to a greater emphasis on the exploitation of culture for profit and accumulation. Since the 1970s and the 1980s, the dominant form of Capitalism, in terms of political-economy, has been Neo-Liberalism. This form of Capitalism has shaped the development of culture — by placing greater and greater emphasis on accumulation and profit as the basis of culture itself. Since the rise of Neo-Liberalism, we have also seen the development of a truly global culture and a truly global society. While this has its positives, in many ways, it also remains the case that Capitalism dominates culture today — both the means of producing culture and the means of enjoying culture. In our society, today, it is increasingly becoming obvious that we need a new form of society and a new form of culture. We cannot predict the future but hopefully the future of society and the future of culture shall be Socialism

— a society based on the social liberation of each and the social liberation of all. In terms of culture, hopefully, we shall see the rise of a liberated culture — a Socialist culture. The best forms of modern culture, since the 1970s, are: Contemporary Art, Modern Art, Situationism, and attempts at Socialist culture. Since the 1950s we have also seen a golden age in the history of literature and the history of writing — leading, possibly, to the formation of a world writing, and a world culture. Hopefully, in the end, Capitalism will be replaced with Socialism.

Notes

1. K. Marx, Capital Vol. I, (1867)
2. V.I. Lenin, Imperialism, (1917)

(2014)

CHAPTER IX

IDEAS AND STRUGGLE: SOCIETY AND CULTURE – A MARXIST STUDY

This essay is a study of society and culture. Culture is part of society. Culture is part of the reality of society. This essay is a Marxist study of the social role of society in the development of culture. This essay is a Marxist study of the need for Socialist culture.

This essay explores the development of culture through the various forms of society which have existed in history and in social development. Culture has developed and has been shaped by the various developing forms of human society. Culture has developed based on the economic and social development of humanity — which produces culture.1

Culture is the social expression of the ideas of human society. Culture is the social product of society. Culture is the product by which people communicate their ideas and persuade others of their ideas. Culture, in Marxist terms, is the social production of the ideas of human society. The study of culture can never be separated from the study of society.2

Culture is the product of all of society. Culture is made by individuals and by groups of people, but the majority of culture is, in the end, the common product of all of human society. Of course, individuals do make culture — but they do not make culture independent of society or independent of each other. Indeed, culture, like history, is made by people — but not always in the historical circumstances that they themselves choose.3 The social basis of culture is vital to understand. It is the social basis of society which creates the basis for culture — for the development of culture and the evolution of culture. It is the social basis of culture, its ability to reflect society and to develop in society, which gives culture its power and its ability to survive and develop. All culture, in the end, can be traced back to the economic development of society and the social development of society. This historical connection between society and culture can never be broken — without destroying either society or culture.

This essay is a Socialist analysis of the role of society in creating the culture of modern society. If we are ever to understand the power of culture, both positive and negative, on human history and human society, we must understand the society which creates it. This society has emerged from social development, economic development, historical development, and cultural development. This fact is obvious, given the ideas of the theory of Historical Materialism — that human history is shaped by material conditions, productive forces, social relations, social struggle, class struggle, and social revolution. It was Marx, himself, who noted that culture, in the end, is the product of society: 'The production of ideas, of conceptions, of consciousness, is at first directly interwoven with the material activity and the material intercourse of men, the language of real life'.4 Marx believed that culture emerges from the interplay between the economic base of society and the ideological superstructure of society. It is in this interplay that produces both society and culture. As Marx, himself, wrote: 'The mode of production of material life conditions the general process of social, political and intellectual life'.5 Society, in the end, determines culture.

Marx's theory of society provides the basis for Marx's theory of culture. Historical Materialism, Marx's theory of society, is the basis for any real theory of culture.

The social basis of society creates the social superstructure of culture. Culture is the product of society. Culture is part of the social superstructure of society.

The economic base of society produces the social superstructure which produces the ideology and the culture of society. This relationship, determined by Historical Materialism, shows the relationship between culture and society.

History and society proceed through several stages of development. These stages of development make up the economic base of society — the mode of production — which creates the social relations that generate culture and ideology.

History and society must progress through certain stages of development in order to achieve social progress. In human history and human society those stages of development and those modes of production are — Primitive Communism, Ancient society, Feudal society, Capitalist society, Socialist society, and Communist society.

The history of the development of human society is the history of the development of humanity through these developments of society. The development of production and productive forces creates the inevitable social development which creates these developments of society.

The economic development of a society is the basis from which all culture and all forms of culture emerge. No form of culture can emerge without some sort of society and some sort of development of society.

The social development of society gives rise to the social development of culture. All of the great cultural revolutions and revolutions in culture have emerged from this fact — from the first societies to the societies of today.

Every major cultural shift and cultural revolution occurred because of the social relations and the social revolutions of society. The cultural power of culture is nothing without the social power of society. Society is the base from which culture emerges and changes.

The illusion of culture is the illusion that culture can change itself by itself. Culture only changes because it is changed by society — by the development of society or by the revolutions of society.

All the best examples of cultural revolution — the Renaissance, the rise of Romanticism, the Industrial Revolution, the French Revolution, the Russian Revolution, the Age of Film, the Revolution of the 1960s, the rise of the Internet — all occurred because of economic developments and social developments. This economic determinism might seem harsh — but it is the truth regarding the overall nature of revolutionary change in culture. Artists might produce revolutions, but it is society which makes those revolutions into permanent revolutions of culture.

Historical development, itself, also shapes culture. Culture divorced from History and Historical development cannot exist — or it cannot exist for long. Historical Materialism, with its ideas about the nature of historical development, shows that culture cannot emerge without some connection to current historical development or some previous historical development. The development of culture is the result of the historical development of society.

The historical development of culture can be summarised by Historical Materialism — as the social development of the ideas of human society.

I. Society and Culture

Humans are social beings. This means that our social progress has usually come from social co-operation. Indeed, the basis of our cultural process has usually come from social co-operation and cultural co-operation. No writer or artist in history, even the most individualistic, has been able to produce truly great art or culture without co-operation with others. Even the basis of our culture comes from some engagement with the culture of the past — in a process of development and refinement which depends on the work of the past. Every piece of art, every piece of culture, is descended from previous ideas and previous developments. The historical nature of culture and art articulates the social reality of culture and art. The co-operative basis of art and culture is the basis for the bulk of human cultural progress and cultural development. As humanity travels into the future the reality of our co-operative culture becomes increasingly apparent — as all of the connections of art and culture become increasingly obvious. The culture of society is the society of culture.

Humanity will always need culture. Humanity will always produce culture. There are few aspects of human nature which do not change across history but the tendency towards producing culture and a need for culture seems to be a constant in human beings and human society. Indeed, it seems that culture and cultural development is a vital part of what makes humanity actually human. The development of culture and society will go on and on until Humanity itself ceases to exist. The various forms of culture which have developed since before the rise of modern society shows the social power of humanity to produce their own culture. Many Socialist writers have pointed to this historical and social ability of humanity — the fact that humans, by their labour, produce both society and culture. This combination, of labour, intelligence, and development, is the basis for all human society and all human culture. If humanity is to survive it will need to always develop its culture and its appreciation for culture. Humanity will always need culture – in order to be truly human.

II. Culture and Society

Human societies produce culture at all levels of society. It is a myth that only the ruling class, in history and in politics, produce culture. Indeed, throughout human history, it has usually been the lower classes, including the working class, who have been vital to the development of culture. Many great artists and great writers came from poor backgrounds. Their work often reflects the social reality behind most types of culture. Their work is often vital, as a revolutionary, tool to change both society and culture for the better. Some of the best working-class people, in history, were those who not only laboured to make a better society but also laboured to produce lasting pieces of art and culture. We can remember all those working-class people who gave rise to many of the best elements of popular culture — who developed a popular culture which was both popular and a culture. Robert Tressell, the great British novelist, was a worker. His novel, 'The Ragged-Trousered Philanthropists' (1914/1955), is one of the greatest novels of the 20th century. It was written by a man who was a sign writer and a decorator, who died of tuberculosis at the age of forty. Tressell's work and Tressell's life shows that a worker can produce culture. Tressell's novel shows that great art can come from any part of society. Their work shows that even the lowest person in society can create a genuine and beautiful piece of culture. The workers produce culture — they produce their own culture which is vital to both society and social progress. As Lenin noted — 'all the marvels of science and the gains of culture belong to all'.6 As C.L.R. James noted — 'every cook can govern the state'.7 Every cook can develop culture and society. Culture, like society, is the development of all. Culture is the development of all. Culture is the responsibility of all.

The working class has been vital to the development of culture and to the revolution of culture. Indeed, the working class has produced the economic base from which all modern culture has emerged. Without the working class there would be no modern culture — as it has been the working class who have struggled to develop the economic development of culture and who have often contributed to culture themselves. The history of culture, from Ancient society to Capitalist society, from the past to today, from class society to the possibility of Socialism, would have been impossible without the countless hours of labour that the working class put into developing both society and culture. The working class are the heroes of culture — both as producers of culture and as developers of culture. All art and all artists are based on the economic developments and economic revolutions which give rise to art and culture. These developments rest on the labour of the working class. If we truly wish to see a new and better culture, we must endeavour to ensure that culture is part of working-class society. The workers can make culture. The workers make society. The workers should be the basis of a better culture – and a better society. Just as the workers are the basis of the development of culture, they are also the basis of the development of a better culture – a free culture.

The dominant form of culture today is Capitalist culture. This means that any serious account of culture must be based on the systematic analysis of Capitalism and Capitalist culture.

We live in a time of crisis. One does not need to be a Marxist to see that Capitalist culture is in crisis today. Indeed, any serious account of Capitalism and Capitalist culture would recognise that both are in serious crisis today. In art, science, religion, economics and ethics, the dominant forms of Capitalist culture are all in decline and are rapidly entering a period of decline. The scale of this crisis is not yet known — but the nature of the crisis which emerged after 2007/2008 seems to show that this crisis will remain a key part of Capitalism for a long period of time. Today there is a crisis in Capitalism. Tomorrow there will be a further crisis in Capitalism.

III. Capitalism and Culture — I

Capitalist culture is in crisis today because it cannot explain the crisis. The sheer scale of the crisis means that Capitalist culture cannot develop any solution to that crisis or any explanation for that crisis. In Historical development those cultures which cannot adapt to crisis — or explain crisis — are usually those cultures which tend to be overturned by crisis — and replaced with new forms of thinking and new forms of society. The fact that Capitalism has been unable to solve these problems is one of the reasons why Capitalism, as the current mode of production, will eventually be replaced by a better mode of production — by a Socialist mode of production. The current nature of the crisis, today, has not yet reached a point where it could overturn Capitalism, or Capitalist culture, but it does suggest major problems for Capitalist culture as it advances into the rest of the 21st century. The scale of the crisis is beyond the explanatory power of Capitalist culture. The scale of the crisis is beyond the ability of Capitalist culture.

The scale of the crisis can be seen in the reality of the major types of Capitalist culture. The level of culture is at its highest in history — but the sheer scale of it means that it cannot solve the major problems facing either

Capitalism or Capitalist culture. The scale of commodification too is a problem — for it essentially means that Capitalism is placing short-term profit ahead of the development of its culture — which will lead to a decline in culture and the culture of Capitalism.

The current decline of Capitalist culture can only be explained by the decline of Capitalism itself. Since the end of the Cold War, it is obvious that Capitalism has entered a new phase and a new period of crisis. This crisis is also universal — it can be seen in all parts of the Capitalist world. This crisis can be seen in the United States, in Europe, in Latin America, in Asia, in Africa, and all the other areas of the world dominated by Capitalism and the culture of Capitalism.

The ideas of Marxism can perhaps explain the crisis of Capitalist culture. The Marxist account for the decline of Capitalist culture is to connect it to the Capitalist crisis of today. It is the crisis of Capitalism itself which has generated a crisis in Capitalist culture. The connection between Capitalism and Capitalist culture shows that a crisis in one causes a crisis in the other. Today we are seeing a major crisis in Capitalism. As a result, we are seeing a major crisis in the culture of Capitalism. The nature of this crisis shows that Capitalism cannot solve its economic problems or its cultural problems. In the long term a new type of society must emerge to replace Capitalism. That new type of society is Socialism.

The problems of Capitalist culture are key problems of Capitalism. Without an operating cultural system, the system of Capitalism is weak. Without the ability to develop its cultural system the system of Capitalism is weak. In many ways this process of development is reflective of a key idea in Historical Materialism — the limits of social development under an existing mode of production. Indeed, at some point in the development of any mode of production that mode of production runs into its own limits — particularly the limits of its ability to develop the forces of production and to maintain the relations of production. This weakness means that every mode of production will, at some point in history, be replaced by a bigger and a better mode of production. Capitalist culture is failing not because of any particular problem of its ideas or its structure — but because Capitalism itself is no longer able to find the means of developing itself, its mode of production, its forces of production, its relations of production, or its ideology, without risking the complete collapse of the system itself. We can see this today in the political sphere and the economic sphere of Capitalism — dominated as both are, today, by crisis. We can see this today in the intellectual sphere and the cultural sphere of Capitalism — which are also dominated by crisis. This all means that we are heading into a new type of crisis and into a new type of development — whether we like it or not. Hopefully, this will all give birth to a better society — to Socialism and a Socialist society.

IV. Capitalism and Culture — II

Capitalist culture, since the 1950s, has continued to develop. It is this culture which still dominates the culture of humanity in most parts of the world. Since the end of the Cold War the expansion of Capitalist culture has been extensive. We could say that the period of Neo-Liberalism, the period since the 1970s and 1990s, has been the period of the global expansion of Capitalist culture. There is not one part of the world which has avoided this expansion of Capitalist culture. Indeed, it is difficult to find any culture, today, which is not Capitalist in one form or another — or does not base its culture and cultural development on the accumulation of profit and the distribution of cultural commodities. As a phenomenon in human history and human society there has never been a period when culture has had such a global reach, and global impact, as today's Capitalist culture. Its reach has impacted the development of culture on all continents and in all countries. As part of human development this development is both positive and negative. It is positive in the sense that it has expanded the power of culture and the means of developing culture. It is positive in the sense that it has created a global world and a global society. It is negative in the sense that it has created monopolies and a monopolistic form of culture. It is negative in the sense that it is a culture which undermines all other forms of human culture and reduces them simply to the process of exploitation and accumulation. If a better society is ever to emerge, we must have the means to understand Capitalist culture and its global impact. The global reach of Capitalist culture is truly global.

Capitalism likes to present itself as a great defender of culture. Capitalism likes to present itself as a great promoter of culture. This is true — when compared to the limits of Ancient culture and Feudal culture. Capitalism has certainly helped to develop the means of production needed to achieve a very high level of culture. Some of the best examples of human culture were produced under Capitalism — or are being produced under Capitalism. The problem, however, is that Capitalism also has the tendency to undermine culture. Capitalism also has the tendency to destroy culture which is not profitable. Capitalism also has the tendency to spark great conflicts and great wars which also destroy culture and bring about a rise in the level of barbarism in human societies. The reality of the First World War and the Second World War, both of which were caused by Capitalism and by Imperialism, should remind us all that Capitalism can often destroy culture. Capitalism is capable of both producing culture and destroying culture. The nature of Imperialism, especially, means that Capitalism is capable of destroying culture which it does not approve of — especially culture which resists it or its attempts to profit from all parts of human society and human culture. The history of anti-Socialism is a history of Capitalism actively crushing politics, societies, and cultures that Capitalism does not approve of — resulting in the deaths of millions. There is a serious contradiction in the history of Capitalism and culture. On the one hand Capitalism has raised the level of production to such an extent that it is now possible for all of humanity to enjoy the benefits of all of human culture — to engage with all of human culture. On the other hand, Capitalism limits culture to only those who can afford it — and exploits the labour of all to pay for it. The limitations of Capitalist culture are shown by the real reality of culture under Capitalism — that only profitable culture is allowed to survive. This means that Capitalism is only interested in profitable culture — and is quite prepared to destroy all other forms of culture to ensure that profit. Capitalism is only interested in profitable culture — not good culture. The history of Capitalism is full of examples of Capitalism destroying parts of human culture. The history of Capitalism is full of examples of Capitalism ignoring that culture that it is not interested in profiting from. If we really want to understand the relationship between Capitalism and culture, then we must remember that Capitalism is not interested in the production of art — Capitalism is interested in the production of commodities. Art and commodities can often be the same thing — but it often means that any form of art which is not a commodity is ignored or destroyed by Capitalism. Capitalism, in its rush to profit from culture and from art, is often the destroyer of culture and art. Capitalism is one of the great creators of culture. Capitalism is one of the greater destroyers of culture. We need a system and a society which values culture — rather than seeks to limit culture to the amount of profit it can generate. We need Socialism.

Capitalism is a system based on exploitation and oppression. Capitalist society will never free itself of its basis as a system of exploitation and oppression. Capitalism is built on a reality of exploitation and oppression. Both of these aspects are built into Capitalism and will remain part of Capitalism until the day it is overcome by Socialism. Capitalism is also, intrinsically, a class society. This means that Capitalism will never be a system based on free development and free association — because it will always maintain the unequal relations between Capitalist and Worker. In order to have a truly free society and a truly free culture we need to have a society which has eliminated exploitation, oppression, and class. This means that Socialism must replace Capitalism. Socialism is the only system which can eliminate exploitation, oppression, and class. Socialism is the basis for a free society. Socialism is the basis for a free culture.

The sheer scale of human society, and the development of human society, has led to an explosion of culture. It has led to an abundance of culture. This explosion of culture has reached a particular turning point in the reality of culture under Capitalism and the reality of Capitalist culture. This reality of culture under Capitalism cannot last forever. It will be replaced by Socialism. The sheer scale of Capitalism means it can produce any type of culture that it wants — and yet Capitalist culture and Capitalist society are undergoing the worst sort of crisis since the crisis of the 1920s, 1930s, and 1940s. Capitalist culture has been morbid for nearly a century and yet it manages to still dominate the means by which culture is produced and distributed. This cannot go on forever. This will not go on forever. Historical Materialism shows that all forms of culture are eventually replaced by new forms of society and new forms of culture. The same will occur to Capitalism and Capitalist culture. Capitalist culture will be replaced, in the long run, by Socialist culture. Capitalism will be replaced, in the long run, by Socialism.

V. Socialism and Culture — I

Socialism will replace Capitalism. Socialist culture will replace Capitalist culture. Socialism will do this because Socialism is a historical development, an economic development, a political development, and a social development. Socialism will achieve a free society which will liberate both humanity and culture.

Socialism is a form of society where the means of production are democratically controlled. Socialism is a society based on co-operation, equality, and the abolition of competition and hierarchy. Socialism, as a new form of society, will give rise to a new form of culture. Socialism will give rise to a culture based on the principle of 'from each according to their abilities, to each according to their needs'. Socialism will give rise to a culture based on the principle of 'the free development of each is the condition for the free development of all'. Socialism will create a new sort of society — based on equality and democracy — and it will create a new sort of culture.

Socialist culture will be good because Socialist society is based on achieving the liberation of humanity, including the culture of humanity. Socialism is based on achieving a democratic society — at all levels of society. This means that Socialism will generate a democratic culture — a culture committed to the democratic expansion of culture and the democratic development of culture. In historical terms, Socialism will give rise to the first culture to truly overcome the limitations of class and class society. Socialism will achieve its own vision of equality for humanity by abolishing class. This will give rise to the countless development of culture itself — as humanity will at last be free to develop culture according to human need, rather than at the whims of a ruling class.

VI. Socialism and Culture — II

Socialism will give rise to a working-class culture. It will give rise to a free culture. The working class, in Capitalist society, produces most culture today — as most artists and thinkers are workers. Socialism will give the working class the ability to truly free their ideas, their work, and their culture from the limits of Capitalist culture and Capitalist society. Instead of the culture of a ruling class there will be a culture of the working class – a culture of human freedom. This culture will be democratic, collective, individual, free, and based on developing the human relationship of community and freedom to greater heights and greater development. The old restrictions on culture, imposed by Class society, will be done away with — and will be replaced by a society which truly values the social use and the social necessity of culture. Socialism will liberate the worker and the artist. Socialism will liberate culture and art. It will make culture truly human – and truly free. This is the Socialist vision of culture. This is the Socialist vision of art.

Socialism will give rise to an international culture. Socialism will unite the world by uniting all of humanity to the social organisation of Socialism — liberating the entire world from both exploitation and oppression, and from class and hierarchy. This will give rise to an international culture based on human solidarity and human freedom. This does not mean that Socialism will eliminate cultural differences between sections of humanity — rather it will eliminate only those differences which maintain exploitation and oppression. Human beings will be free to enjoy their own languages, literatures, and cultures — but they will also be free to enjoy other cultures. They will be free to develop a human culture, one which is international in its vision and its scope. Socialism, at the cultural level, has no desire to force humanity to adopt a single culture — rather it frees humanity to develop its culture with respect and solidarity. Socialism will liberate all cultures and allow them to develop in a human and humanistic way. Socialism will liberate the culture of America, Europe, Africa, Asia, and Oceania, and allow the Workers of those continents to develop their culture in Freedom, Respect and Solidarity. This means that all cultures will develop, and all cultures will unite. The achievement of a single Socialist world will bring about both a world culture, an international culture, and a human culture. It will bring about an explosion of individual culture, collective culture, and social culture. The great cultural vision of Socialism is the vision of both a world with an international culture and a world of respected local culture. Socialism is based on a very basic vision and a very basic principle — 'workers of the world, unite'.

VII. Development and Culture

The development of society, towards Socialism, necessitates thinking about the nature of culture. We need to be able to concretely show the connection between society and culture in order to transform both society and culture to achieve a free society — a Socialist society. We cannot simply assume the connections between society and culture. We cannot believe that society and culture are unconnected. Society is a social development itself. Culture is not ahistorical — it develops depending on its historical development, its economic development, its social development, and its social circumstances. Socialist culture cannot be imposed on society — it must develop, organically, from society itself. This is why it is impossible to think about Socialist culture without thinking about Socialist society. This is why it is impossible to think about Capitalist culture without thinking about Capitalist society. Society precedes culture. Development precedes consciousness. Things precede words. Humanity develops its society before it develops its ideas about society. Marx understood this in his understanding of social development and historical development – in the form of his theory of Historical Materialism. Specifically, he understood that art and culture is a product of history and of society. He also understood that art and culture, in the end, is a product of society. Art is not an abstract product of society but a real, historical, social, and human product of social relations of society. Art, in the end, is not an abstraction but part of the real concrete development of social progress. Marx outlined this, in a section of the

Introduction to the 'Grundrisse' (1857):

> The object of art, like any other product, creates an artistic and beauty-enjoying public. Production thus produces not only an object for the individual, but also an individual for the object.8

The development of culture is part of the historical development of material production. This means that art and artistic development, in the end, is connected to social development. Every artistic development and revolution are a product of wider social development. The renaissances of art, throughout history, are the product of social revolution.

When humanity looks back at the history of culture and the history of society it will see many successes and many disasters. The point, however, is to struggle for a better society and a better world. This sort of approach guarantees that humanity will respect its past — but will also struggle to achieve a better future.

People make their own history and their own culture — but they do not make it outside of history. If we wish to see a better society and a better culture, we cannot reject the entire legacy of the past — or we will fail. Instead, we need to build a better society, and a free society, on top of the old. A free society, and a free culture, needs to emerge from the crises and failures of Capitalist society and Capitalist culture.

The main problems of Capitalist culture are economic and cultural. The economic problem is that Capitalist culture depends on profit and accumulation. This means that the development of Capitalist culture depends on economic profit — rather than the development of culture itself. The cultural problem is that Capitalist culture is becoming increasingly unable to develop itself. Much of Capitalist culture is stuck in the limits of Capitalism itself. Even American culture, the basis of Capitalist culture today, is finding that it has economic problems and cultural problems. The inability of Capitalist culture to escape its economic and cultural problems means that Capitalist culture is heading for crisis — both economic crisis and cultural crisis. This level of crisis is obvious today — when we look at the reality of the development of Capitalist culture since the end of the Cold War and the beginning of the crisis of 2008. The Capitalist system can no longer afford to develop its culture. The Capitalist system can no longer maintain the development of its culture. The result of this will be crisis — at some level or another — within the system of Capitalism and within the system of Capitalist culture. The sheer level of Capitalist culture, today, is overwhelming but it cannot even solve the simplest problems in regard to its ideas and its development. Capitalist culture, today, is a static culture. Static cultures tend to die or collapse. Capitalist culture, today, cannot solve its economic problems or its cultural problems.

A major problem of Capitalist culture, today, is that it has no direction. Capitalist culture has no real idea of where it is going — and has lacked such direction since the end of the Cold War. This has resulted in the reality that Capitalist culture lacks both focus and direction. The core ideas of Capitalist culture, particularly American culture, are unable to adapt to the changing reality of Capitalism itself. Of course, Capitalism can still profit from its culture, but it is no longer able to really develop it. The crisis at the centre of Capitalist culture is a crisis of direction, a crisis of production, and a crisis of reaction. The sheer commodification of culture in Capitalism today means that Capitalism is unable to really develop its ideas without subjecting them to immediate profit. The short-term nature of Capitalism means that new ideas, and the new development of new ideas, are impossible. In cultural terms Capitalism is now only really capable of repeating itself— or appropriating from earlier periods of cultural development. Capitalism, today, is vampire-like in that it can only develop its culture by appropriating from the past or by appropriating from the present. These problems of Capitalist culture have been obvious since the 1930s — and have only increased in difficulty since the end of the Cold War. Consumerism might produce profit for Capitalism, but it can no longer produce a revolution in culture. The limits of Capitalist culture are increasingly being reached — just as Capitalism itself has managed to reach its geographical and economic limits. Capitalism might survive — even for a century — but it will not be able to solve its economic problems or its cultural problems. The problems of Capitalism and Capitalist culture will only continue to develop — until the day that Capitalism is replaced by Socialism. The final crisis of Capitalism will come about due to economic problems — but it will also come about due to social problems and cultural problems. The working class will overthrow Capitalism, not simply for economic reasons or political reasons — but because they alone have the power to produce a revolution in society and a revolution in culture. The working class, alone, can free us from the problems of Capitalist culture.9

The sheer level of the current crisis of Capitalism means that Capitalism will probably reach a further level of crisis. The current crisis, as it has developed since 2008, shows that Capitalism itself can no longer afford the Neo-Liberal phase of Capitalism. This means that change will have to come to Capitalism — and to the culture of Capitalism. Capitalism, itself, due to its interests, will resist this change — and it will resist it with further social crisis and further social disaster. The level of crisis in Capitalist society, today, means that culture itself feels the effects of crisis. This will lead to the development of culture — but it will also mean that culture will become increasingly trapped within the limits of Capitalist society. The limits of Capitalist society will ultimately undermine Capitalist culture — leading to social change and social revolution. Capitalism and Capitalist culture will fall in the end — and they will be replaced by Socialism and Socialist culture.10

VIII. Future of Culture — I

Capitalist society and Capitalist culture cannot free humanity or human society. They have both achieved progress for humanity and human society — but they are reaching their historical, cultural, and political limits. It is time for humanity to think about replacing Capitalism and Capitalist culture. It is time for humanity to think about alternatives to Capitalism. The alternative to Capitalism is Socialism. Marx predicted that social struggles lead to either 'the revolutionary reconstitution of society at large or in the common ruin of the contending classes'. In our world, today, we are faced by this choice — the choice between Socialism and Barbarism. If we continue on with Capitalism and Capitalist culture, we might reach a point where Barbarism will triumph — leading to the end of humanity and the end of human civilisation. If we want to prevent this, we must build a better society — we must build Socialism. Marx's prediction and Marx's warning has been reinforced by history. Every time humanity reached a point of crisis it led either to revolution or counter-revolution, to a new society or to barbarism. This is the simple choice we find ourselves in today — between Capitalism and Socialism, between no world or a better world. Humanity has reached a major crossroads today. Our choice is the choice between Capitalism and Socialism. Our choice today, our only choice, is the choice between Capitalism and Socialism. We must choose Socialism. There is no future but Socialism. There is no other future but Socialism.

IX. Future of Culture — II

The future of Capitalism will probably be a future of crisis. This future will impact the future of culture under Capitalism. Capitalism will attempt to solve its own economic problems and social problems by blaming its failing culture. Indeed, most supporters of Capitalism base their critiques of contemporary society on culture — rather than economic reality, political reality, or social reality. The fact that Capitalism cannot solve its problems leads it to blame its own culture — because to blame its economics, its politics, or its overall social structure, would be to blame the entirety of Capitalism itself — and Capitalism cannot develop such critiques of itself. All this means that Capitalist culture will probably become increasingly monopolised and dull — in the reality of the Capitalist State and the reality of Capitalist society. Supporters of Capitalism will probably attempt to ignore such developments — or blame their increasing cultural and social problems on the Left. One of the great ironies for the future of Capitalist culture is that despite having absolute control over the direction of social culture and political culture since the 1980s, Capitalism has been unable to prevent a crisis of Capitalism itself. The crisis of Capitalism is not only a crisis of Capitalism as a social system. It is a crisis of Capitalism as a cultural system. The history of Capitalist culture is full of examples of this type of social crisis leading to major cultural crisis — such as during the 1930s and the 1960s. If history is any guide Capitalism will be unable to solve the current problems of Capitalism — including its cultural problems. The future of Capitalist culture is a future of crisis.

We must replace Capitalism with what Socialists call 'social humanity'. Marx, in the 'Theses on Feuerbach' (1845), specifically Thesis X, showed that the focus of humanity should be to replace 'civil society' with 'social humanity': 'The standpoint of the old materialism is civil society; the standpoint of the new is human society, or social humanity'. We need to replace Capitalism with a society which is not only an economic society but a cultural society and a social society. A society in which all will have access to culture. A society in which all will be able to develop culture. That sort of society is Socialism.

Socialists want a free humanity. We want a 'full life' for all human beings. This is one of the key ideas of Socialism — to provide and develop the 'full life' for every member of every community. This sort of society can only emerge through Socialism. It cannot emerge in any other way.

It is impossible to fully outline what Socialist culture will be like. This is because it is utterly utopian to try and outline Socialism in advance of the victory of Socialism. What we can know is that Socialism will be a democratic society. What we can know is that Socialist culture will be a democratic culture. The working class with its economic society of Socialism will create a cultural society of Socialism. This is the hope of

Socialism and the hope of culture.11

X. Hopes of Culture

The working class is capable of culture. The working class is capable of making both its own culture and a new culture. Any engagement with the history of the working class and the history of the working-class movement shows that the working class can develop culture to new heights and new developments. The working class are not philistines of culture — indeed, they are some of the best producers of culture. The working class are the class which can create both a better culture and a Socialist culture. Their ability to do this is shown by history and by politics — along with the history of culture and the politics of culture. In political terms the working class has only achieved great things for culture — because it is both a producer of culture and a consumer of culture. Nearly every development of modern culture and modern art has been shaped by the work and taste of the working class. In democratic terms the working class alone has the social power and the political power to achieve a truly democratic culture — because they are the majority — both at national levels and international levels. This level of cultural power and political power is unprecedented in the history of culture. It means that the working class has the power to completely transform both society and culture — if they struggle to change society. Socialism, in many ways, will be about liberating the working class and society — but it will also be about liberating culture and placing it firmly in the democratic hands of the working class. This is a truly revolutionary development in the history of society and culture. The revolution of Socialism will be a revolution of culture. In place of class society, we will have a classless society. In place of class culture, we will have a creative culture. In place of an oppressed culture, we will have a free culture. The social revolution which this transformation represents is an impressive one. It represents the first time in human history where culture will be purely in the hands of the majority. This majority will be able to use this culture to develop both culture and society in any way they see fit. This will be a true revolution in every sense of the word. The revolution of Socialism will bring about a real revolution of culture.12

XI. Socialist Culture

There is a real need for Socialism. There is a real need for Socialist culture. Socialism does not emerge because it is a moral or ethical idea — it emerges because of history and the development of society. Socialism is moral and ethical — but the historical force of social revolution is the real reason why Socialism will be achieved in the future. The power of Socialism to change both our society, and ourselves, is one of the most powerful social forces in the history of humanity. We can compare this power, in cultural terms, to the Renaissance. The Renaissance marked the beginning of the end of the Middle Ages and the beginning of humanity's freedom from Feudalism. This was a major victory in the history of human society and human development. The victory of the Renaissance brought about a revolution in human society and human culture. The victory of Socialism will do the same. The victory of Socialism will bring about a revolution in human society and human culture. The victory of Socialism will be a new Renaissance — a new birth of freedom and a new birth of culture. We need Socialism not only to solve the economic and political problems of our times — but also the social problems of our times. We need Socialism and a Socialist society to achieve a further revolution in arts, society, and culture. Socialism will bring about a Renaissance in arts, society, and culture, because Socialism alone has the social power to bring about the liberation of all of society — for every man, woman, child, and person. In the struggle for Socialism, we are also struggling for a new society and a new culture. The liberation of Socialism is also the liberation of culture. Only with Socialism and Humanism will we achieve a better society. Only with Socialism and Humanism will we achieve a better culture.13

XII. Realities of Culture

The future of culture cannot be predicted. Instead, we should struggle to ensure that the future of culture and the future of society is a future based on humanity, humanism, and Socialism. The struggle of a better culture can only occur if we build a better society. Even if a better culture emerges from Capitalism, it will be useless unless all can share it. Humanity cannot produce culture which remains simply the property of a privileged few and a privileged elite. Culture is the birth-right of all of us. Culture is the concern of all of us. We all deserve culture.14 We all deserve to have access to culture. We all deserve to have the chance to expand culture. We all deserve to have the chance to contribute to culture. The duty of any Socialist is to make Socialism — but it is also the duty of any Socialist to make a society which is better for all. This means struggling to ensure not only the development of culture but full access to culture. We should all struggle to live in a world where the culture of the past and culture of the future is known to all. We should all struggle to ensure that culture is part of the common culture of all.15

The future of culture is not certain. It might collapse or be re-born. The hope of the future of culture is also an expression of the hope of the future of society — that all can enjoy it, that all can experience it, that all can take part in it. The building of Socialism is the building of a human culture. The building of Socialism is the building of social humanity.

Notes

1. C. Caudwell, Studies in a Dying Culture, (1938)
2. C. Caudwell, Studies in a Dying Culture, (1938)
3. K. Marx, The Eighteenth Brumaire of Louis Bonaparte, (1852)
4. K. Marx, The German Ideology, (1845)
5. K. Marx, Preface to a Contribution to the Critique of Political Economy, (1859)
6. V.I. Lenin, Summing-Up Speech at the Third All-Russia Congress of Soviets of Workers', Soldiers', and Peasants' Deputies, (1918)
7. C.L.R. James, Every Cook Can Govern, (1956)
8. K. Marx, Foundations of a Critique of Political Economy, (1857-1858)
9. M. Horkheimer and T. Adorno, Dialectic of Enlightenment (1947)
10. M. Horkheimer and T. Adorno, Dialectic of Enlightenment (1947)
11. M. Horkheimer and T. Adorno, Dialectic of Enlightenment (1947)
12. R. Williams, Culture and Society, (1958)
13. R. Williams, Culture and Society, (1958)
14. R. Williams, Culture and Society, (1958)
15. K. Marx and F. Engels, The Communist Manifesto, (1848)

(2016)

CHAPTER X

SOCIETY AND LITERATURE – A MARXIST STUDY

This essay is a study of literature. Literature is part of society. Literature is part of the culture of society. This essay is a Marxist study of literature under Capitalism. This essay is a Marxist study of the need for Socialist literature.

Literature is part of any serious social revolution or intellectual revolution. If we look at the history of society, and the history of literature, we can see that literature and writing has always been vital to the social struggle for social revolution. Every revolution, and every revolutionary movement, has produced its own literature — its own revolutionary literature. This means that literature, in its various forms, is a real revolutionary force — both in history and in the world today. If we are to ever really understand the history of culture, and the continuing development of culture, for revolutionary politics and for revolutionary struggle, then we must understand literature. We must try to write a revolutionary literature. We must try to build a revolutionary literature.

Writing was one of the key social revolutions of human history. Human beings have been creating writing and literature since the rise of urban societies — following the Urban Revolution.1 Writing was a revolutionary development in the history of humanity — a major social revolution.2 Writing remains crucial to the development of any serious form of social revolution today — such as Socialism. As long as human civilisation exists, today, writing will be a crucial and revolutionary part of it. As a form of culture, writing is also the form of culture which has most shaped our ability to remember culture itself. Writing, as a tool of humanity, is a crucial revolutionary tool. Writing helps to make revolution possible in human societies. It allows revolutions to both develop ideas and to express ideas. Indeed, it is impossible to make revolution without a revolutionary literature.

This essay is made up of seven sections. Each of these sections deals with a specific area relating to the relationship between society and literature. Literature is about writing and ideas. Literature is a historical development. Literature is a revolutionary development. The history of literature is connected to the politics of society and the culture of society. If we wish to change society and culture, we must seek to develop a better literature — alongside social change and social revolution. Literature is the basis of both thinking about the world and the basis of changing the world.

I. Literature and Society

All societies produce literature. All societies produce writers. Good literature is a social part of any good society. Good literature is also a political part of any good society. As humanity has progressed, both in history and in development, literature has become a key part of the reality of humanity. Since the invention of writing, at the time of the urban revolution, humans have used writing to both record ideas and to develop ideas. Every advance in human society has brought about an advance in literature or a revolution in literature. Literature and society are connected. Every writer, and every literary writer, knows that they and their work are connected to society. Every writer, and every social writer, knows that their work is shaped by society. Today the major forms of literature are still shaped by society and by the struggles of society. Since the 19th century there are essentially two types of literature in the world — Capitalist literature and Socialist literature. Every serious writer who engages with the world, today, understands that their choice of literature is a choice between Capitalism or Socialism. Every major writer today either writes for Capitalism or writes for Socialism. This is the social reality and the political reality of writing today — in modern Capitalist society. The full effect of society and social struggles on writing can be felt today — as writers struggle to engage with our times and our changing times. Literature remains a vital way of both understanding society — and changing society. The revolutionary nature and the revolutionary development of literature links literature firmly to the possibilities of revolution and social revolution. In the struggle for Socialism today literature is a vital part of both interpreting the world and changing the world. Literature is a crucial part of the struggle for a better world and a Socialist world. Literature is a crucial part of the struggle for Socialism.

Literature is part of modern society. Literature has always been part of the social struggle of modern society. Literature has always been part of modern society. Literature has always been part of the struggle for a better society. All of this means that literature is crucial to making a better world today. Reading and writing, as a revolutionary force, are crucial to building a free humanity.

Society, today, is a literary society. With the advance of literacy, reading, and writing, most of modern society has been shaped by literature – by the power of reading and writing. More and more people, in modern society, can read and write. More and more people, in the modern world, can engage with literature. More and more ordinary people have access to reading and writing. This social reality is a powerful force in modern society. It is a powerful force which can change the world.

Literature is a social force. Literature as a social force is necessarily part of society and its social background. No writer can escape their social background and their society. No writer can escape the politics of their times — or their own politics. Culture, today, reflects that social base and political base that has produced it. Capitalism, and Capitalist society, has produced the majority of culture and literature found in the world today — either in support of it or in opposition to it. The idea that 'the ruling ideas are the ideas of the ruling class', in the words of Marx, is an idea that can be easily applied to literature and the ideas of literature. The ruling literature is the literature of the ruling class. Prior to Capitalism this relationship of writing and ruling-class culture was very obvious too, between writing and Feudalism, between writing and the Ancient World. Today, most writing is formed by its society — by Capitalism, by Capitalist society, by the Capitalist base of society and the Capitalist superstructure. Most literature, today, is affected by Capitalism and Capitalist ideas. Indeed, Capitalism is the social basis for almost all literature which exists today. This is the political and social background of most literature today and most literature written over the past two centuries — as it has been since the Industrial Revolution and the 19th century heights of bourgeois culture. Today, literature, both political and non-political, is often part of Capitalism and Capitalist society — either to support it or to oppose it. Literature is social. Literature is political. This means that we need to think of literature as a social force if we are to really understand its role in society today.

Literature is a revolutionary force. Literature tells us a great deal about the revolutions and counter-revolutions of society. Literature tells us a great deal about society itself. All types of society produce their own form of literature — from Ancient society to Feudal society to Capitalist society to

Socialist society. Indeed, literature was a key part of the Long Revolution which produced the transition from Feudalism to Capitalism (1450-1850). Modern literature, alongside the revolution of print and the revolution of the printing press, emerged alongside early Capitalist society — after the 1500s and after the 1600s. The age of Shakespeare, Milton, Swift, and Defoe, was also a revolutionary period which saw the rise of Capitalism – in Britain. The novel, itself, as a major form of literature, also emerged out of the rise of Capitalism. Indeed, the novel, as a major form of literature, really emerged during the same period as the rise of Industrial Capitalism. Capitalism and Modern Literature emerged together and developed together — as humanity struggled to move beyond the limits of Feudal society. This shows the revolutionary link between literature and society. This shows how literature tells us something about the reality of society. This revolutionary nature of literature remains part of society today. Literature is still a major revolutionary force in society.

Modern society has produced a powerful literary culture. Modern society has produced many great writers. Many of these writers were revolutionary writers – writers who engaged with the revolutions of their times. Many of these writers were produced by revolution. In the case of Britain, the first major industrial Capitalist state, the revolution of Capitalist industry transformed British writing over a century. In the case of France, the Revolution of 1789 generated a new type of French literature and saw the birth of modern French literature. During the 20th century the American novel, as part of advancing Capitalist development in the United States, transformed human writing — and became a crucial part of the modern culture of Capitalism. The development of Capitalist society also gave rise to Left literature and Socialist literature. From the 1800s we can see the emergence of solid left-wing writing — which sparked further revolutions in writing. The development of Socialist literature also gave rise to the development of social novels and political novels — particularly the work of Orwell. Today the vast development of writing has only increased — as new ways of writing and new revolutions of writing continue to be developed within modern society. The power of writing to spark social revolution or to support social revolution has also developed since the emergence of modern society. It is impossible to think of any major social revolution or political revolution — in the last two centuries — which has not generated a revolution in writing or a revolution in literature. The revolutionary power of literature is an obvious power and an obvious result of the modern relationship between revolution and literature. This revolutionary power is a social power. Capitalist society has transformed culture, sometimes for the better, sometimes for the worse. Capitalist culture, and Capitalist writing, is now in decline. The politics of writing today is often determined by that fact. Politically and culturally, Capitalist society has reached a fin de siècle known as neo-liberalism — and all writing, all political writing, all serious literary writing, today, is reflective of this despairing and exhausted reality of Capitalist society. In our own period of crisis, as Capitalism enters the 21st century, the choice between Capitalism and Socialism once again emerges — not simply as a political and economic question, but as a social and cultural question. One that determines the future of literature as an exercise of human creativity. Writing, today, is either for the preservation of Capitalist culture — or the attempt to construct a new, better, Socialist culture.

Society produces literature. In the end the type of literature which emerges, in any society, is the result of the society which creates it. A Capitalist society produces Capitalist literature — generally. A Socialist society produces Socialist literature — generally. A Socialist society might yet produce not only Socialist literature, but also a better society. Socialist society needs to produce both better literature and a better society. It is on this basis that Socialism might yet be able to achieve a better form of culture.

Society, today, is a Capitalist society. This means that it is a society which is dominated by the reality of Capitalism – specifically, exploitation and oppression. Clearly, we need a better society today – a society which is free from exploitation and oppression. Socialism, a society based on the free development of each and the free development of all, is what is needed today. We need Socialism. In order to achieve Socialism, we need to change society. In order to change society, we need to struggle – and we also need ideas. Literature, as a revolutionary force, can help to develop the revolutionary ideas we need to change society – to create a better society.

The struggle in literature today is the struggle for Socialism and for a Socialist literature. Socialism is a society based on the principles of the free development of each and the free development of all. Only Socialism can create the type of society which can truly free literature and writing. Only Socialism can create the type of society which can truly achieve an educated society — and a liberated society.

Socialist literature needs to be developed — if Capitalist literature is to be challenged. In order to develop Socialist literature, we must first understand what Capitalism does to literature. In order to develop a Socialist literature, we must struggle for a Socialist literature. This means that Socialist literature, fundamentally, is a product of the need for social struggle. Socialist literature, because it is produced by struggle, is part of the struggle for human liberation.

II. Capitalism and Literature

Capitalism is a society based on private control of production. It is a society based on exploitation and oppression of workers – by a Capitalist class. Capitalist politics, and Capitalist hegemony, has shaped the development of literature and the development of writing. Capitalist politics and Capitalist hegemony over the past two and a half centuries, globally, has ensured that the majority of culture in the culture of society today, even in global society, has been determined by Capitalist politics and Capitalist hegemony. Literature, as part of the history of ideas and the history of culture, has not escaped from the dynamic of Capitalism — instead, it has become a vital and contributing part of it. Ever since the rise of Capitalism, literature has been a key part of Capitalist society.3 Capitalist society has created its own culture: Capitalist culture. Capitalist hegemony has helped to create a Capitalist culture. Capitalist culture has helped to create Capitalist literature. Capitalist hegemony, and Capitalist culture, has played a powerful role in the historical development of Western culture since 1800.4

Capitalism has produced modern literature. Capitalist society and Capitalist culture, since the 1800s, has had a powerful impact on the course of writing — both in history and in politics. Most of the culture and literature of the past two centuries has developed from this economic and political reality of Capitalist society and Capitalist culture — following the relationship between base and superstructure. This has produced a very powerful written and literary aspect to Capitalist culture, simply via the successes of Capitalist society over the past two hundred years — alongside its failures and difficulties. The result has been the importance of literature and writing in the wider culture of Capitalism — of writing both as a commodity and as an expression of ideas. Literature, today, is heavily connected to Capitalism.5

Capitalism took a long time to emerge – between 1450 and 1850. It took a Long Revolution for Capitalism to triumph in the modern world. The rise of Capitalist literature was a Long Revolution. This Long Revolution of culture took centuries to develop, certainly in Britain and France, yet it provided the intellectual basis of modern society. This has impacted the development of both Capitalism and Socialism. The Long Revolution, today, is the long struggle for human freedom – for Socialism.6

Capitalist literature is limiting. Capitalist literature is interested only in profit. In the end Capitalist literature cannot challenge the ideas of today which justify exploitation and oppression. Capitalist literature was an excellent contribution to the history of literature — but it is no longer a revolutionary type of literature. The struggle for literature, today, is the struggle to overcome the limits of Capitalist literature — and to replace it with a better form of literature.7 A Socialist literature is needed today.8

III. Socialism and Literature

Socialism is a society based on the free development of each and the free development of all. Socialism emerges from the problems of Capitalism. Socialism, as a social and political movement, emerged in the 19th century – and became a major political force in the 20th century. It is a movement based on the struggle of the working class – as the majority of humanity. It is a movement based on the struggle to free and liberate all of humanity – to achieve the free development of each and the free development of all. Socialism, specifically, emerges from the real struggle to achieve a better world. Socialism, objectively, is about building a free, democratic, and humanist world. Socialism, as an intellectual movement, has also been a literary movement – producing some of the greatest writers and thinkers of the last two centuries. Indeed, some of the best writing in human history has been Socialist writing – writing which argues for Socialism, writing which struggles for Socialism. Socialist writers tend to be radical writers – writers who understand the importance of writing to social struggle, and to the struggle for a better world. They tend to be writers who are involved in social struggle. Socialism has not yet been achieved in modern society – despite two centuries of struggle – but it still remains a crucial part of modern politics, and modern writing. Today, in our own times, Socialist writing is a powerful force – arguing for a new, and better, society – against Totalitarianism and for Democratic Socialism.9

Socialism needs writing. Socialism needs writing because education and ideas are vital to the struggle for a better society. Socialism can only succeed in the struggle to liberate the world from Capitalism, when it is capable of producing ideas, politics, and writing. Socialism needs writers and Socialism needs writing.

Socialist writers have been vital to the history of literature and the history of Writing. Socialist writing, like most Socialist Parties, and Left parties, tends to produce a lot of writers and writing. This writing often differs, greatly, in its quality, but the bulk of that writing is vital to understanding the history, politics and personalities of both Socialists and Socialist Parties. Socialist writers, both in and outside their Parties, both in and outside of politics, produced a great deal of material in the 20th century. This material was crucial to the development of Socialism, but it also helped to develop a Socialist culture — a culture which reinforces the ideal of a society based on the free development of each and the free development of all. Socialist writers, today, continue to produce a great deal of material. This writing varies in its style and genre — from politics to autobiography, from literature to history, from theory to journalism. If any serious history of Socialism and Socialists is ever to be written it will have to deal with Socialist writing and Socialist writers. Writing is vital for Socialism.10

A Socialist writer tends to be a political writer. A Socialist writer tends to be dedicated to the political struggle for Socialism. Socialist writers tend to be dedicated, both politically and as writers, to their politics and their writing. They tend to try to produce work quickly — both for immediate politics and for immediate questions of theory. They also tend to try to make their work relevant — as part of the wider social struggle for Socialism. Their expression, and their work, varies but tends to be grounded in politics and political language. They tend to reject the limits of genre and style for immediate politics and political thought. They tend to be of a very high standard. They also tend to produce work across genres — from politics to history, from economics to philosophy, from fiction to nonfiction. As a type of writer, the Socialist writer is a dedicated writer.

The Socialist writer, and the Socialist thinker, is a political writer. It is the politics and the political dedication of the Socialist writer and the Socialist thinker which make the Socialist writer and Socialist thinker capable of changing the world.

The task of the writer is to write. The task of the writer, in society, is to write. The task of the Socialist writer is also to write — but to also outline Socialist thought and Socialist visions within their literature. This is a political task, but all writing is, in one form or another, political and has its political tasks. No writer can escape this political reality — even the most apolitical and apathetic. Writing is political — as George Orwell pointed out. Orwell, as a Socialist writer, always understood that the struggle for literature is a political struggle and a social struggle. Orwell always understood the importance of developing a Socialist literature. Writing is part of the Revolution. Writing is part of the Socialist Revolution.11

IV. History and Literature

Literature has a long history. The history of literature is the history of society. The history of literature is the history of literature both reacting to society and changing society — with its ideas and its writing. This ensures that literature forms part of the real development of modern history and modern society. Modern social change, and social change in history, cannot be effectively understood without reference to literature and writing. This is why literature is so vital for understanding modern society and modern history. This is why literature is crucial to understanding the history of humanity. This is true for all types and pieces of literature.12

The history of modern literature is connected to the history of modern society and the history of modern revolution. The transition between various forms of society, from ancient society to feudalism, from feudalism to Capitalism, from Capitalism to Socialism, has also defined literature and writing.

The development of literature is a historical development. It is important to understand that literature — as a cultural form — has been shaped by social development and by social struggle. The revolutions and counter-revolutions of human history have shaped and determined the structure of literature — just as the individual work of individual writers has shaped the development of literature.

The development of literature cannot be divorced from history. Indeed, history is a form of literature — especially in the recording of history. If we are to ever understand historical development and historical struggle, we must understand the development of literature itself. The writer can be an actor in history and the history of literature — just as the lives and biographies of countless writers and countless authors also show throughout the development of history and writing.

Writing is a social process. The history of writing is the history of literature alongside the history of social struggle and social development. If we are to understand the pace of human history, we must understand human literature and human writing. The history of literature is the history of society. The history of literature is the history of revolution.

V. Revolution and Literature

Literature is a crucial part of social revolution. Every social revolution, in history, has produced literary revolutions – revolutions in writing, revolutions in reading, revolutions in literature. In order to really understand the social impact of literature we must understand that literature is a revolutionary force. Literature, since the rise of writing itself, during the time of the Urban Revolution, and the first urban societies, has been crucial to every major social and political revolution in human history. Literature has not only shaped revolution it has helped to create revolution. Literature has ensured that revolutions not only have revolutionary ideas, but also have the means to express those revolutionary ideas. Every major development in social revolution has always produced a major development in literary revolution.

The rise of the social revolution of mass literacy, during the Industrial Revolution, has produced the basis of both Capitalist society and Socialist society. This revolution has produced an audience for writing and people capable of writing. The rise of modern society and modern industry also gave birth to an explosion of diversity in writing — from workers, from peasants, from women, and from the marginalised. The rise of the novel, in literature and in society, during the seventeenth, eighteenth and nineteenth centuries, reflect stages of this social revolution — through literature. This revolution in literature eventually produced further social revolutions. Today, the social results of mass literacy also show how vital mass literacy is to social revolution.

Social Revolution tends to produce Intellectual Revolution. Intellectual Revolution tends to produce Literary Revolution. It is Literary Revolution which tends to produce the best new types of writing. No writer has been able to write without engaging with the reality of the socially-generated and socially-created ideas which surround them. Every Intellectual Revolution in the modern world, from the beginning of industrial society, has contributed to the thought, the ideas, and the writings of every modern writer. Every writer is the product of the mass of social revolutions and intellectual revolutions produced by modern society. In intellectual terms every writer is the product of both social revolutions and intellectual revolutions. Every writer, in one way or another, is a product of revolution.

The history of revolution is the history of the development of literature. Every major social revolution and political revolution produced its own forms of literature. The English Revolution, the American Revolution, the French Revolution, the Russian Revolution, the Chinese Revolution, the Cuban Revolution, and all other revolutions, produced their own writing and their own literature. This literature allowed these revolutions to occur — but it also allowed these revolutions to change the world, by producing a means of spreading their ideas across the world. It is impossible to separate revolution from literature. It is impossible to separate literature from revolution.

Revolutions always produce revolutionary writing. It is impossible to study revolutions without engaging with their writing and their literature. Every revolution needs to be studied through the literature it produced. This literature not only explores the ideas of revolution — but also the social struggles of revolution.

Revolutionary literature is good literature. Sometimes it is great literature. Indeed, some of the best writing, in human history, was produced by revolution – by revolutionary writers. The English Revolution unleashed the writings of John Milton. The American Revolution shaped the writings of Thomas Paine. The French Revolution inspired Byron and Shelley. The Russian Revolution produced Soviet fiction, Soviet science-fiction, and the best, first-wave, novels of Socialist realism. Revolutions in society also produce revolutions in literature. Some of this literature is the best literature that humanity has produced – so far.

Today the only possible revolution in literature is a Socialist Revolution. This is because only a Socialist Revolution in literature can produce a revolutionary change in literature. Only a Socialist Revolution can produce as great a revolutionary change in literature today as the one produced by the Capitalist Revolution of the 1500s-1800s. Literature needs revolutions in order to maintain itself and to develop itself. Literature needs Socialist Revolution. This is also because only Socialism can produce both the technical revolution and intellectual revolution to produce a revolution in literature itself today. There is also the fact that Capitalism itself, as an established form of society, can no longer produce revolutionary changes to culture on the scale that it produced in the past — even with the rise of the internet. Today the choice for literature is a simple one — a choice between Socialism and the continuation of a stagnant Capitalist culture.

VI. Crisis and Literature

Capitalism, historically and politically, always reaches points of crisis — like any class society. This crisis affects and shapes literature too. This nature of crisis in Capitalist society can be approached in two ways in the literary field: either as a threat to literature or a revolutionary struggle for it. In the earlier periods of crisis in the history of Capitalism a similar process has always occurred.

Capitalism is connected to crisis. Indeed, Capitalism is based on crisis. Social crisis and social revolution tend to produce the best forms of Literature. Social crisis and social revolution tend to force authors to think about society itself. Capitalism is in crisis today. This crisis of Capitalism has been evident since the 2000s — and especially since the crisis of 2007/2008. This crisis has affected literature and affected the development of literature. This crisis has also produced major problems for literature. The crisis has generated the basis for a better literature to emerge — a literature which can challenge Capitalism and take part in overthrowing Capitalism. The history of literature is full of examples of where crisis produces the basis for revolution — for revolutions in literature. It is time to think about developing a better literature — a literature which can challenge both Capitalist society and Capitalism itself. It is time to develop a revolutionary literature. It is time to develop a Socialist literature.

Any writer, alive today, can see that the political crisis of Capitalism has produced a cultural crisis of Capitalism. This means that literature has been affected by the wider crisis — just as all crises tend to shape literature. Today, every writer needs to write about the reality of the crisis of Capitalism and how it is affecting modern human society. This is a simple fact of being relevant to any discussion about humanity and the world today. Of course, writers can write about whatever they wish, but the crisis of today demands that writers engage with the reality of the crisis — even if it is just to acknowledge that we are all living in a reality of crisis.

The crisis of Capitalism, today, means that every writer must engage with the political reality of crisis. Indeed, every writer of fiction or nonfiction is probably engaged with the reality of the crisis today — simply as a reality of their work. This means that every writer has to pick a political side, in terms of their writing. They can write either for Capitalism or Socialism. A writer can either write for counter-revolution or for revolution. A writer can either write for Barbarism or for Socialism. This is the political choice facing every writer. This is the social choice facing every writer.

Literature, in the early 21st century, has entered an interesting social period. This period has been shaped by Neo-Liberalism. It is a difficult period for Left writing and even Left literature in general. In the last few decades, first and foremost, many of the best aspects of literature and writing have been limited by the reality of Capitalist culture — as Neo-Liberalism has clearly changed modern society. Literature, in the past few decades, has been undermined as a critical force by Capitalist society. Literature, today, needs to be critical of Capitalism. It needs to be critical of Neo-Liberalism. Literature can only be really critical of Capitalism when it is a Socialist literature. Literature, in the 21st century, really needs to be a Socialist literature.

Social crisis and social revolution tend to produce the best forms of literature. Social crisis and social revolution tend to force authors to think about society itself. It is usually in the context of social crisis and social revolution that the best literature is produced. The best literature, in the end, is revolutionary literature.

Capitalist society, today, has clearly developed a series of problems. These problems have been created by a series of crises. Capitalist culture, itself, is in crisis today. This is because of the crisis of Capitalism itself today. The crisis of Capitalism is clearly having an effect on literature. The history of Capitalism is full of examples of crisis shaping the development of literature — e.g. the 1840s, the 1930s, and the 1960s. That reality of crisis has certainly re-emerged today. Capitalism is in crisis — and it is producing a crisis of literature.

The crisis of Capitalism is producing a crisis of literature. It is possible that this crisis will become a revolutionary crisis and a revolutionary struggle — both in literature and in society.

VII. Literature and Socialist Theory

Writing, simply as a record of history, politics, society, and culture, has been vital to all societies — including modern society. This means that writing is socially powerful. This means that Socialists have to engage with the power of writing – in the struggle for a better world. There is a need for a Socialist theory of literature. There is a need for a Socialist theory of writing. If we can understand the power and reality of writing, in theoretical terms, we can perhaps use writing as a really revolutionary force in society. This means that the development of a theory of literature is crucial for Socialism – and for Socialist politics. Literature, and the study of literature, is a powerful part of Socialist theory.

The development of Marxist literary theory — from Georg Lukács to Raymond Williams — provides the basis for thinking about the relationship between society and literature. This is especially important for thinking about the revolutionary power of literature.

The Socialist theory of literature focuses on the politics and social relationships of literature. The best examples of this Socialist theory of literature remains Lukács' 'The Historical Novel' (1937), written during his Russian exile in the 1930s, and Williams' 'Culture and Society' (1958), written and published in the 1950s. The key argument of these two Socialist writers was simple: that literature is both social and political, both socially determined and politically determined. The Socialist analysis of literature is that literature is social and political. The key point of Socialist analysis of literature is: the social basis of literature, the economic basis of literature, the political basis of literature. For Socialists, literature is always a social product of society. Lukács applied this method and this idea to the political novels and historical novels produced at the height of the great bourgeois culture of the 19th century. Williams applied this method and idea to the literary culture of Capitalism, and the literary culture of emerging Late-Capitalism. Williams also applied it to the Long Revolution which produced bourgeois culture and bourgeois literature in the three centuries after the end of Feudalism — between 1450 and 1850. Indeed, Williams argued that the Long Revolution of the 19th century, specifically both the Industrial Revolution and the Democratic Revolution, was crucial to the development of the ideas of Socialism. Raymond believed that if Socialism is to be established – via Socialist Revolution – Socialism requires both Industrial Revolution and Democratic Revolution, both economic development and democratic development. Socialism, as the free development of each and the free development of all, must emerge from both economic revolution, democratic revolution, and social revolution. Both Lukács and Williams applied a Socialist analysis to Capitalist literature. Both Lukács and Williams helped in the development of a Socialist literature. Within our current political and cultural period, that of the early 21st century, the concept that literature is both social and political can be applied to the reality of human cultural progress through economic and social progress — and through economic and social revolution. This is the basis of all Socialist ideas about literature today — society shapes literature, literature shapes society, revolution changes society and literature. Literature, like all culture, in the end, is advanced by the process of social revolution. If literature is to advance, today, we need social revolution – e.g. Socialism.

VIII. Socialist Literature and Socialist Politics

The social struggle, today, is between Capitalism and Socialism. The literary struggle, today, is between Capitalism and Socialism. We need Socialism and Socialist literature in the struggle for Socialism. There is an increasing need for a new Socialist literature — one which describes current society in Socialist terms and in literary terms. There is an increasing need for Socialist literature to both interpret society and to change society. All these points, necessarily, show the need for a Socialist literature. A Socialist literature can only be produced by Socialist writers.

Socialism, today, has a powerful literary tradition. Socialist writing really produced its first real Socialist literature in the 19th century and in the 20th century. It was in the modern era, after the Industrial Revolution, and the rise of the working class, that Socialist writing became a really powerful literary force. In the 19th century we can see the emergence of French Utopian Socialist novels, British Socialist poets, left-wing Russian novels, American protest journalism, and the first novels dedicated to the struggle of the working class. We also see the first working-class writers. The social novel became a literary force in the 19th century. In the 20th century these traditions expanded and were joined by new types of literature — from the revolutionary novel to the literary critique of modern Capitalism. The rise of this Socialist literature was connected, completely, to the rise of Socialism as a social movement – and with the rise of the possibility of a Socialist society. From this emerged the social power of Socialist writing – in the form of Socialist literature. In the same period, we can also see the development of new, powerful, forms of writing – protest novels, working-class novels, proletarian novels. In the long years of the 20th century the development of Socialist novels and Socialist writing continued on into new genres and new forms, and produced some of the best pieces of literature in human history — from Steinbeck to Orwell, from Tolstoy to Marquez. Today, Socialist writers are still producing excellent work — a Socialist literature. Today Socialist writers are still struggling for a better society.

Socialist writers understand the connection between society and ideas. George Orwell was a Socialist and a Socialist novelist. He understood, better than most, the importance of society and ideas in literature. His writing also showed the means of combining society and ideas in literature — towards a Socialist literature. The objective of any piece of Socialist literature, in the end, is to further the cause of Socialism — to help in the practical achievement of Socialism. A Socialist writer, ultimately, dreams of the day when humanity, by abolishing class, will be free to both write literature and create literature on a free and equal basis. Orwell understood that literature, as a political and social force, will be vital to any liberation of humanity. He also understood that literature will be vital to protecting humanity from counter-revolution.

In conclusion — there is a need to think through the problems of Socialist literature. There is a need for a Socialist literature and a need to understand Capitalist literature. Marx, Lenin, Trotsky, and Gramsci, all noted the importance of Socialist literature in the creation of a Socialist politics, a Socialist society, and a Socialist hegemony. Socialist literature is vital for not simply understanding Capitalism — but also for overthrowing Capitalism. Socialism is the basis of real liberty — and real liberty is the basis of real culture and real literature for all.13

Orwell, an excellent Socialist novelist, made the point, long ago, that all literature is political, and that all writing is political. He was, of course, correct. Essentially all good writing is political. As a result, all Socialist literature cannot help but be political by its very nature. This includes all genres and all styles, all writing and all literature, all political writing, and all political ideas.14 All writing can serve the cause of Socialism.15

We need to see literature as its own social force — a force that is capable of changing society in real, revolutionary, terms. Literature is part of society and part of a changing society.16 Literature is part of society today. Literature is part of the struggle between Capitalism and Socialism.17 Literature is part of the struggle to achieve Socialism.18 Literature and Capitalism must be replaced by literature and Socialism.

Notes

1. V. G. Childe, Man Makes Himself, (1936)
2. V. G. Childe, Man Makes Himself, (1936)
3. G. Lukács, The Historical Novel, (1937)
4. R. Williams, Culture and Society, (1958)

5. R. Williams, Culture and Society, (1958)
6. R. Williams, The Long Revolution, (1961)
7. B. Anderson, Imagined Communities, (1983)
8. M. Gorky, Untimely Thoughts, (1917-1918)
9 G. Orwell, Why I Write, (1946)
10. R. Williams, Marxism and Literature, (1977)
11. G. Orwell, Why I Write, (1946)
12. G. Lukács, History and Class Consciousness, (1923)
13. C. Caudwell, Studies in a Dying Culture, (1938)
14. R. Williams, Marxism and Literature, (1977)
15. T. Eagleton, Marxism and Literary Criticism, (1976)
16. R. Williams, The Long Revolution, (1961)
17. R. Williams, Marxism and Literature, (1977)
18. R. Williams, Marxism and Literature, (1977)

(2014)

CHAPTER XI

SOCIAL WRITERS

This short essay is a study of social writers. Social writers are writers who write about society. Social writing is about challenging society – through writing about society. One of the great literary developments of the 19th century and of the 20th century, it could be argued, was the rise of the social writer and the rise of the social novel. In those two centuries we start to see the emergence of a new type of writer and a new type of novel — the social writer and the social novel. The social writer writes about society – in order to change society. The social novel is writing which directly engages with social developments and social realities — in order to challenge the modern world. The social writer, and the social novel, directly engages with society — and attempts to change it. Of course, all writers have engaged with social developments and social realities, in history, but it was not until the 19th century that writers began to seriously challenge the social reality of society — both in fiction and in non-fiction. Social writing is one of the most powerful forms of writing today. It has the power to both interpret the world and change the world. Good writers can produce revolutions. Good social writers can produce social revolutions.

Social writing is writing about society. It is writing which tries to look at the real problems and issues of society. It is writing which tries to change society – by inspiring radical change. It is writing which can be either fiction or non-fiction – but it is always critical. It is writing which tries to examine the real problems of society – economic problems, social problems, political problems, etc. It is writing which tries to argue for the need for a better society. The best type of social writing is writing which tries to argue for Socialism – for a democratic society based on human freedom. It is writing which ultimately tries to struggle for a better world. A social writer, as a writer, is someone who uses writing to explore the problems of society – while also arguing for the struggle for a free humanity. Social writing, as a form of writing, is about society – in order to improve society.

Social writing is clearly a major literary force. Some of the best examples of modern writing, in the past two centuries, have been social novels – novels which engage with modern society and its problems. Most of the great modern classic novels which we still read today, in modern society, are social novels – novels which engage with society, novels which explore the problems of society. When we think of the best novels, today, they tend to be novels which are about society and humanity – about the nature of society, the nature of humanity, and the possibility of human freedom. The best novels tend to be about society – rather than just about individuals. A good writer, today, tends to be a social writer – a writer who is interested in human society, a writer who is interested in changing society for the better.

Social writing is also a major social force. Social writers have often played a key role in changing society – as their ideas are read by large numbers of people, in the form of essays, articles, short stories, and novels. Social writers can reach society. The best social writers can reach millions of people. In terms of social struggles and politics, the social writer usually sells more books and is more influential for society, for culture, and for politics, than the author of dry academic books. That influence is social, and it is political. It is an influence that can help to shape society and social struggle. It can change the world. Of course, influence does not mean action — but influence can result in action. If we are interested in the struggle for a better world today, and a Socialist world, then social writing can help towards the struggle.

Social writing is both a political style and literary style. Indeed, it is the most political and most social literary style in literature. It is a style of writing which tries to combine politics with literary writing – in order to use writing to change the world. It is the best writing style of our times — because it challenges us to challenge our society. It challenges us to interpret our society. It challenges us to change our society. It is also a very modern style — because it engages with modern society.

Social writing tends to be Left writing. Social novels tend to have Left politics. The struggle for social change usually places the politics of the social novel on the Left. There are Right social writers — but a social writer, today, is usually a Left writer. Social writers tend to want to change the world. This means that a social writer is usually a Left writer. This fact is clearly the case for most of the great social novels produced in the last two centuries. When we look at the majority of truly great social writers or social novelists most came from the Left, or firmly from the Socialist Left. In many cases most of their best work was produced when they were most clearly engaged with the politics of the Left and the ideas of the Left. Orwell's novels, for example, were always Left novels — novels based on Left politics. This was the case in both the social novels of Orwell and the more political novels of Orwell. In the end the best type of Left novel has come from the social writer — either as social novels or as political novels.

The goal of serious writing is to change the world. The project of most social writers is to change social conditions. The project of the social novel, to interpret the world, and to change the world, has been a key part of the social project of social novels since the beginning, and has remained part of the project of the social novel ever since — into the social novels of the 20th century and the current century. People usually write social novels, in the end, because they want to change the world – by exposing the problems of society.

Social writing is a modern literary development. It is a form of writing which really emerged in modern society – after the Industrial Revolution. The modern social novel, for example, first began to emerge in modern writing with the rise of modern society in the 19th century and in the 20th century — novels about society, novels about changing society. The publication of Dickens' 'Hard Times' (1854) and Hugo's 'Les Misérables' (1865) mark the beginning of the social novel as a form of writing. The publication of the work of Zola and Tressell marks the arrival of the left-wing social novel. Most countries and most societies, since the 19th century and since the 20th century, have produced their own social writers and social writing. In Europe and America, social writers have been a major radical literary movement — producing some of the best literature of the past two centuries, from Tressell to Saramago. In Britain, this movement resulted in Tressell and Orwell. In Russia, this movement produced Gorky and Tolstoy. In the United States this movement resulted in London, Steinbeck, and Sinclair. In Latin America it produced the great social novelists like Marquez and Galeano. In Asia it produced writers like Lu Xun and Takiji Kobayashi. In Africa it produced writers like Ngugi wa Thiong'o and Nadine Gordimer. For women writers, the movement of social writing was particularly wonderful — producing figures like the Brontës, George Eliot, Woolf, Lessing, Le Sueur, and Le Guin. For African Americans, and their long struggle for freedom in the 19th century, the 20th century, and today, the movement of social writing produced writers like McKay and Baldwin. Social writing also produced the most important literary writers of the 20th century – writers like George Orwell, Jack London, Upton Sinclair, Ernest

Hemingway, M.A. Sholokhov, Albert Camus, and Graham Greene. The result of the literary development of social writers and social writing is the reality of social writers and social writing — the attempt by writers to understand society and change society, through literature and writing. The emergence of the social writer and social writing generated not only new ways to think about the world, to see society as it really is, but also revolutionary ideas to change the world itself.

Social writers engage with society. They are writers who write about society – in order to change society. Social writing, and the social novel, is a literary form of using writing to engage with society and social developments — with class, with poverty, with social problems, with gender, with race, with social structure, with social revolution. Plots and characters, structure and text, ideas, and ideals, all of these elements in social writing engage with wider society in the form of the social novel and in the form of the social writer. For the social writer, the reality of society, as it is developing in the real world, is the social basis for their work — especially their literary work. The social writer engages with society and with social developments. The social writer always engages with the classes, the structure, the culture, the politics, the successes, and the failures, of their society — in order to change their society.

Social writers are political writers. Most social writers engage with writing about society for political reasons — either to expose and explore the problems of society or to argue for a change in society. Social writers also tend to write about society in order to politically change society – in order to help build a better society. Most social writers, today, are left-wing writers – and most of them are inspired by the politics of Socialism. This is because social writers, as political writers, want to change the world – and the politics of the Left are about trying to change the world for the better. Many of the best Left writers of fiction, in the last two centuries, have specialised in social writing — through critical writing, through radical writing, through revolutionary writing, through social novels. Indeed, some of the best Socialist writing of the last two centuries came in the form of the social novel — such as Orwell's novels on Britain in the 1930s and 1940s or Steinbeck's novels on California.

The 20th century was a key period for social writing. Indeed, writing in the 20th century was largely defined by social writing. Every major social event of the 20th century, every major change in society, every major political revolution, and every major social revolution, produced social writing and social novels about it. In many ways social writing, and social novels, clearly helped to shape the politics of the 20th century. The 20th century, itself, as a revolutionary century, also inspired social writing – writing which challenged existing Capitalist society. Indeed, every social event in the 20th century inspired work by social writers. Events like the First World War, the Second World War, the Great Depression, the Spanish Civil War, and the Russian Revolution, helped to inspire major writers – major social writers. These events also clearly shaped the politics and hopes of most of the great writers of the 20th century – especially writers like Orwell and Hemingway. The social revolutions of the 1960s and 1970s, and the counter-revolutions of the 1980s and 1990s, also produced their own social novels. In the 20th century most of the truly great examples of literature were usually examples of social writing – writing about society, writing about changing society, writing about the hopes and fears of society. In the end, the importance of social writing and social writers can be seen across most of the writing produced by the 20th century — a century of revolution and a century of writing. Today, in the 21st century, the social writer remains a key source for understanding what happened in the revolutionary 20th century. In the 20th century, social writing was clearly important.1

Social writing, as a writing style, can be applied to any society. The social novel can be applied to any society. Indeed, when we look at the novels produced in the 20th century, we find social novels appearing in most places and most times. The social novel is a universal type of novel. Its structure and its type can be found anywhere where there is a literary tradition and anywhere where there are committed social writers prepared to write about society in a radical way. The rise of Left politics in the 20th century, and their continuing struggles, perhaps accounts for this. The social novel, as a genre, might have started in Industrial Europe — but it has become a universal genre. It has spread across the world — from the Americas to Asia, from Africa to Oceania. The social novel, and the social writer, has also managed to become a key part of many national traditions of literature. In Japan, Takiji Kobayashi's 'The Crab Cannery Ship' (1929) is still read — as a classic, as a political classic, as a Socialist classic, and as a social protest of Japanese society. In China, Lu Xun is still the major national writer. In the United States, Steinbeck is still the most recognised writer of the 20th century. In Britain, Orwell, the greatest writer of the 20th century, is now remembered as the greatest modern British writer. Left writers tend to be remembered as the best national writers. This is perhaps odd, especially when those writers might have been hated and dismissed in their own times, either as revolutionaries or as radicals, but it is a testament of their strength as writers — and the effective nature of their work. Social writers, and social novels, often triumph over other types of writers and novels — simply because they are good writers and good novels, and because they reflect something about our society and ourselves. There is also the case that the social writer can become a national hero or an international hero — because of the brilliance of their writing and the brilliance of their work in reflecting the social reality of their society. Steinbeck remains the greatest modern American writer. Orwell remains the national writer of modern Britain.

The most important type of social writing is the social novel. Social novels are novels of social critique and social revolution. They are novels which examine the problems of society – through fiction. The structure of the social novel often revolves around understanding a social problem — class, poverty, gender, racism, social problems, exploitation, oppression, revolution, etc – and using that understanding to argue for a better society. Everything in a social novel is ultimately connected to examining social problems and the problems of society. From this emerges the basis of the social novel as the novel of social protest. The great social novels which deal with social conditions (Sinclair's 'The Jungle', Steinbeck's 'Grapes of Wrath', Farrell's 'Studs Lonigan', Dickens' 'Hard Times', Orwell's 'Keep the Aspidistra Flying', Charlotte Brontë's 'Shirley', etc.) revolve, ultimately, around exploring the universal problems of society and the social problems of society. As novels they work because they are about society. For the social novel, the social scene is almost the main character of the novel itself — the basis of the plot, the basis of its social criticism, and the basis of its social action. For a social novel, society is the real basis from which the social novel rises as a novel.

Writing is important, in political terms, but writing has to inspire action to be useful. Writing has to inspire action in order to be really useful for social change. Unless it can inspire politics, inspire the masses, and achieve political change, then writing is usually boring, static, and useless. A social novel is always written with the goal of changing the world. A social writer always writes with the hope that their work will change the world. The social purpose of social writing is to expose social problems, in order to inspire the struggle for social change. This applies to most of the great social writers of the past — from Steinbeck to Orwell, from London to Hemingway, from Sinclair to Farrell, from Tressell to Marquez, from Eliot to Gordimer, from Sartre to Camus, from McKay to Baldwin. All of these writers became writers because they wanted to change the world. Orwell's work, in particular, always fits this idea. Orwell, as a writer, wanted to use writing to actively change the world. Indeed, he wanted to make 'political writing' a 'political art'. Writing, however, is only one part of changing the world – the other part is to struggle to change the world. Orwell always understood that writing is always part of the more important task of achieving social change — of achieving political change. The novel is useless unless it achieves change. The social novel is useless if it is ignored. Every serious social writer, both in the past and today, understands the goal of social writing is always about achieving serious social change: a better world.

Social writers can inspire change. They can inspire change through their writing, their ability, and their actions. This is the real power of the social writer. A good social novel makes people aware of the problems of their society – and forces them to engage with their society. A really good social novel, which understands and criticises society, can inspire social struggle – specifically, social struggle for a better world. A really powerful social novel can even force people to change society. Novels, and writing, do not change the world by themselves – but the best novels can inspire people to change the world. This is the real power of writing. This is the real power of the social writer.

Social writers can inspire other writers. They can inspire radical writers. Of course, writers inspire other writers but the specific role of social writing inspiring other radical writers is very important — both in social terms, political terms, and literary terms. Social writers, as radical writers, can inspire other writers to engage with the same radical ideas – specifically ideas to change society. A truly great social writer inspires people to struggle – but they can also inspire other writers to write about radical ideas. Writers like Orwell, London, and Hemingway, for example, clearly have inspired other radical writers. Often this inspiration can last for decades – and inspire other forms of social writing. The great American social novels of the 1930s, for example, owe much to Sinclair's earlier social novels in the 1900s. The novels of the British Left in the 20th century, in one way or another, were often inspired by Tressell and his masterpiece — 'The Ragged-Trousered Philanthropists' (1914/1955).2 Writers inspire writers. Social writers tend to inspire other social writers.

The social novel and the social writer can also inspire other types of writers. The novelist inspires other novelists, but the social writer can inspire other types of writers. The historian, the political theorist, the sociologist, the investigative reporter, the activist, all of these specialist types of writing and research can be inspired by social writing — even if it is to test whether the account of the social problem in the social novel was true or not. The political nature of protest novels ensures that many writers can be hesitant to acknowledge their debts to the social novel — but they are often there, if only in the style and the nature of the content of their work. Political writing, in Britain and elsewhere, owes more than it can say to Orwell — from his political journalism to his political novels, from his social novels to his Socialism.3

Can social writers and social novels change politics? Can they change the world? Indeed, there are examples of novels changing society and politics. There have been many historical examples where social novels, and social writers, have changed history. Sinclair's 'The Jungle' (1906), for example, changed the nature of American food production and forced the American government to create the Food and Drug Administration (FDA). Chernyshevsky's novel 'What is to be Done?' (1863) clearly inspired Lenin. Lenin named his great book about the revolutionary party 'What is to be Done?' (1902) after the novel. Novelists can fight and struggle for social change – as shown by Orwell and his struggle against Fascism and for Democratic Socialism. Novelists can also inspire political change after their own deaths. Takiji Kobayashi, the Japanese Communist novelist, was murdered by the Japanese police in 1933 but his novel, 'The Crab Cannery Ship' (1929), remains the greatest novel ever written on the subject of labour strikes – and it remains the great classic novel of the Japanese Left. At the very least the social writer and the social novel can inspire change, if not exactly create change in direct political terms. Social writers and social novels influence politics — even if they do not always create politics.

Orwell is probably the greatest social writer. Indeed, Orwell was probably the greatest writer of the 20th century.4 His work has always been impressive — even in his day, even if he gained his fame only when he was close to his own death. Of course, Orwell was a political writer — he was a Socialist — but he was also a social writer. His social works, such as 'The Road to Wigan Pier' (1937) and 'Down and Out in Paris and London' (1933), are as important as his political works, such as 'Homage to Catalonia', (1938) 'Animal Farm' (1945), and 'Nineteen Eighty-Four' (1949).5 His journalism was also both social and political. His criticisms of Stalinism, Imperialism, and Capitalism were excellent – alongside his defence of Democratic Socialism. Orwell, the greatest Socialist writer and novelist of the 20th century, cannot be ignored. He remains the greatest social writer of the 20th century who actually developed politics. He was also correct in political terms: if there is any hope for the future, it lies with the working class.

What is the social role of thc social writer today? Of course, the basic role of the writer is to write — to produce ideas, to produce essays, to produce books. Yet the role of the social writer is more than this. The social writer looks at existing society, tries to explain it, and tries to find ways of changing and improving it. Social writers, by their writing, take part in the struggle for a better form of writing, but also in the struggle for a better world. This is essentially what a social writer does and what a social writer attempts to do.

Social writing remains powerful – and important. The goal of the social writer remains powerful today: to understand society and to achieve change — to change the world. Social writers try to interpret the world and change the world. Marx's great saying, after all, was that we should both interpret the world and change the world. The emergence of the social writer and social writing helped in both these struggles — both to interpret the world and to change the world. Writing and literature, today, is a political force — it is also a social force. Social writing is a force for Socialism. Social writing is a force for human freedom.

Are there many social writers writing today? Indeed, there are. There are many. They are writing. They are writing about social crisis, political crisis, economic crisis, and cultural crisis in the world of today. In political terms the social writer is a key social force — writing about society's problems and seeing not simply those social problems but also ways to solve them. The role of the social writer is to write — but their role is also to develop ideas which might help achieve a better society. In political terms this is crucial, as many of the best Left writers of the last century made clear. If social progress is to be achieved, today, it will rely not only on understanding the problems of today and fighting for solutions — but also on creating a much deeper sense of humanity. If we can create a better sense of humanity, through writing and struggle, we might achieve a free humanity – a Socialist humanity. Indeed, if a Socialist society is ever achieved it will still rely on its writers and its artists —just like it relies on workers. The writer can help to build Socialism. The writer can help to inspire Socialism. The social writer can help to build a better world.

The social novel is a great genre. Indeed, it is the greatest genre of modern literature. Of course, however, the social novel is not a perfect genre. Nothing is ever perfect – especially writing. Indeed, the social novel always has its limits — as all literary forms and literary genres do. Indeed, the very nature of the social novel, as a novel of social observation and social criticism, can produce literary drawbacks as well as literary advances. Many social novels can be poor examples of literature. Many social novels can miss the point and the mark. Many social novels can end up being rubbish. Many social novels can end up being counter-productive — despite their commitments and despite their sincerity. Many of the Socialist Realist novels, written in the 1930s and 1940s, in the Soviet Union, for example, have their merits — but they are also products of Stalinism and most of them clearly supported the politics of Stalinism rather than the liberating politics of Socialism. There is also the reality of the social novelist turning against their ideals and their work — as happened to John Dos Passos, author of the truly great 'U.S.A. Trilogy' (1930, 1932, and 1936). A good social novelist might begin as a Socialist and become a Conservative — but the opposite is also true, and a Socialist writer can often remain a Socialist. Orwell, the greatest social writer, was a Socialist — and he remained a Socialist, despite the legacy of Stalinism and the legacy of the Cold War.6 There is also the problem of political action: the fact that books, by themselves, cannot achieve political action. A novel might inspire politics, but it can never make politics by itself. In the end the novel remains just a novel. There are always limits to how far a book, even the most radical, well-written, or expressive book, can really change the world. A book can change the world, but in the end, it is people and their actions which ultimately change the world. A book can inspire change, but a book does not make social change itself. Even the most important book in modern history, the Communist Manifesto by Marx and Engels, did not make history by itself – because it is always real, living, people who make history in the end. Social change, in the end, is achieved by the people — and by revolution. If we want to change the world, we must change the world ourselves.

Social writing still helps to change the world. Life and writing are not the same — but social writing matters.

Notes

1. W. Benjamin, The Author as Producer, (1970)
2. R. Tressell, The Ragged-Trousered Philanthropists, (1914, 1955).
3. G. Orwell, Homage to Catalonia, (1938)
4. G. Orwell, Why I Write, (1946)
5. G. Orwell, Nineteen Eighty-Four, (1949)
6. G. Orwell, Nineteen Eighty-Four, (1949)

(2014)

CHAPTER XII

SOCIALIST WRITERS

This short essay is a study of Socialist writers – the role writers play in the struggle for Socialism. Writing is a major part of the struggle for Socialism in modern society. In the struggle for Socialism there have been many Socialist writers — both writers of fiction and writers of non-fiction. Socialism is a movement, and a struggle, but it is also a movement which needs ideas – and writing. The struggle for Socialism needs its writers. The struggle for Socialism needs its writing.

Writing is central to Socialism. Every Socialist movement has produced writers. Every struggle for Socialism has produced great writers. Every development in the history of Socialism and the politics of Socialism has produced Socialist writers. The history of Socialism is impossible to write without acknowledging the ideas and struggles of Socialist writers. Socialism, as a society based on the principle of the free development of each and the free development of all, is a society which needs literacy – the ability to read and to write. Socialism, itself, will be a society where every member of the human race will be able to read, to write, and to enjoy writing. Socialism is development plus workers' power. Socialism is also literacy plus workers' power.

Socialism is a working-class movement. Writers are part of the working class. Most writers have to engage with the reality of Capitalist society — and most writers are exploited by Capitalism in one form or another. Socialism, as a working-class movement, requires its working-class writers — simply in terms of developing the struggle for Socialism.

In political terms, Socialism needs writers — writers capable of developing the ideas of Socialism. This is not limited by genre or by the division between fiction and non-fiction. Socialist writers have written about every subject that exists. Socialist writers have written fiction and non-fiction. They have written about science, history, politics, art, culture, theory, practice, and about every other subject which exists in society today. Indeed, some of the best writing, in the last two hundred years, has often been writing by Socialists.

Writing is a vital part of the political struggle for Socialism because it helps to express the ideas of Socialism — both in theory and in practice. Without writing there cannot be either Socialism or the struggle for Socialism. As Maxim Gorky said: 'Just as science is the intellect of the world, art is its soul'.1

Writing is important. Writers have helped to shape history and to shape ideas. The best writers, in the end, can change the world. This is why writers are vital for Socialism – they help to make the argument for Socialism.

Writers help to develop both the theory of Socialism and the practice of Socialism. Writers help to develop the culture of Socialism and the politics of Socialism. Indeed, there cannot really be any struggle for Socialism without ideas. Lenin pointed this out in his famous statement: 'without a revolutionary theory there cannot be a revolutionary movement'.2

The working class has produced many great writers. Indeed, many of the best Socialist writers were members of the working class — from Tressell to Ostrovsky, from working-class literature to working-class poetry.3 The working class has always produced its own writing and its own culture. To deny the fact that the working class has an active voice in the development of culture is to deny reality — the working class have always produced writing and they have always produced some of the best Socialist writing. Today there are many working-class writers — actively working for Socialism, for a better society, and for a better world. Their work is crucial to the struggle for Socialism.

Humanity needs culture in order to be human. Culture is a common social basis to our humanity. Every human being needs culture in order to be human. Capitalist society, with its classes and its class antagonisms, denies culture to the vast majority of humanity. Under Socialism, culture will become part of every human experience and every human experience will become part of culture. The democratisation of society, under Socialism, will generate the democratisation of culture. It will, for the first time, place all of human culture within the hands of all of humanity — allowing the development of a higher level of culture. The role of the Socialist writer in the development of such a new culture and such a new society will be crucial. The Socialist writer will be part of both the struggle for Socialism and the victory of Socialism. The Socialist writer will be part of both the struggle for a new culture and the victory of a new culture.

The struggle for Socialism is not only for a new society but for a new culture. This culture will require writers — writers capable of expressing, in clear terms, all of the new ideas, concepts, and feelings that Socialism will generate. In a society in which the 'free development of each is the condition for the free development of all' there will probably be an explosion in new culture and new developments — indeed, the working class, in its struggles, has already produced some aspects of this new culture.4 As humanity progresses forward, into the future, it will have to record its new ideas, its new hopes, and its new feelings. The social role of the writer will change in such circumstances. Rather than recording the daily misery of Capitalism and of class society, the writer will be free to explore all the frontiers of culture — a culture which is free and free for all. Under Socialism, culture will not simply be the property of the rich and the powerful — it will be the right and the experience of all. Socialism will make this new culture possible — and it will do so by liberating humanity from class society. This will mean an explosion in both the quality and quantity of writing – and of readers and writers. The victory of Socialism is the victory of culture. The victory of culture is the victory of Socialism.

George Orwell is perhaps the best example of a Socialist writer. He was a writer who excelled in both fiction and non-fiction. He was a writer who dedicated his life both to writing and to Socialism. His novels and his essays are not just examples of good Socialist literature: they are examples of great literature. Orwell was probably the greatest writer of the 20th century. Orwell was certainly the best political writer of the 20th century. Orwell was certainly the best Socialist writer of the 20th century. Orwell perhaps outlined the Socialist duty of the Socialist writer: 'Every line of serious work that I have written since 1936 has been written, directly or indirectly, against totalitarianism and for Democratic Socialism, as I understand it'.5 The duty of the Socialist writer is to write against Capitalism and for Socialism. The duty of the Socialist writer is to tell the truth and to struggle for the truth. Their duty is to write for Democratic Socialism.

The role of the Socialist writer is crucial in the struggle for Socialism. If we are to achieve Socialism, we must have Socialist ideas. Socialist writers, both of fiction and non-fiction, help in the production of those Socialist ideas. With ideas, and with theory, we can begin the struggle for Socialism.

Lenin, a century ago, made the point that revolution is key to the creation of any form of new revolutionary society — but that creation has to be made in a revolutionary way. He also made the point that culture is also key to the making of any new society. He made the argument, multiple times, that in order to achieve Socialism we must also achieve a new, higher, form of culture — in the process of creating Socialism. Lenin believed we could make a new culture via Socialism — in a new revolutionary way. In order to make a new culture we must make that culture in a revolutionary way — via revolution.6

The struggle for Socialism will go on until Socialism triumphs. This means that there will always be a need to develop the ideas of Socialism. Socialist writers are vital in this regard. Socialist writers are vital to the struggle for Socialism.

The struggle of the Socialist writer is to express Socialist ideas and to develop Socialist ideas. This is a crucial struggle. It is a struggle which will help to make Socialism possible. It is a struggle which will make Socialism really human.

Notes

1. M. Gorky, Untimely Thoughts, (1917-1918)
2. V.I. Lenin, What is to be Done?, (1902)
3. R. Tressell, The Ragged Trousered Philanthropists, (1914 and 1955)
N. Ostrovsky, How the Steel Was Tempered, (1932-1934, 1936)
M.A. Sholokhov, And Quietly Flows the Don, (1928-1940, 1934)
4. K. Marx and F. Engels, The Communist Manifesto, (1848)
5. G. Orwell, Why I Write, (1946)
6. V.I. Lenin, Our Revolution, (1923)

(2017)

CHAPTER XIII

CULTURE AND CAPITALISM – A MARXIST STUDY

This essay is a study of culture and Capitalism. This essay is a history of culture under Capitalism. Capitalism, as an economic system and as a social system, emerged out of the decline and fall of Feudalism — particularly after the 1600s, the 1700s, and the 1800s. With the emergence of Capitalism came the emergence of Capitalist culture and the emergence of culture under Capitalism. After the triumph of the Industrial Revolution, Capitalism became a global system and a global force. This meant that Capitalism also became a force capable of creating and generating its own culture and its own forms of culture. With the decline of Feudalism, Capitalism set out to develop its own culture and its own cultural values — culture and values which stood in opposition to the culture and values which developed under Feudalism. These social developments were linked to economic developments, but they were also linked to the rise of the capitalist class as the ruling class of Capitalist society. Capitalism generated its own culture and with it came its own forms of both producing culture and reproducing culture. In terms of economic development, social development, and human development, the rise of Capitalist culture has proved to be a major historical success — in that it completely overcame the limits of Feudal culture, developed its own culture, revolutionised culture, and exported that culture to all parts of the world. Indeed, Capitalism was once a very revolutionary movement in human history, producing the ability of humanity to, hopefully, one day, achieve Socialism. Capitalism is, essentially, the only major economic system in the world today and this economic system has produced one of the most powerful cultures in the history of humanity.1

Capitalism has a simple history regarding culture. Capitalism has been both a revolutionary force and a counter-revolutionary force for culture. Capitalism, like all types of society, developed its own culture – as part of the historical development of Capitalism. Capitalism developed culture beyond the limits of Feudalism — but Capitalism also limited culture to the limits of Capitalism itself. Capitalism has helped to revolutionise culture and to develop culture. Capitalism has also undermined culture and restricted culture. This contradictory reality of culture under Capitalism shows that the political reality of culture under Capitalism is one of profit, commodification, and accumulation. Capitalism helps to develop culture, but it only does so when it is profitable. Capitalism helps to distribute culture, but it only does so when it is in line with the needs of Capitalism. Any analysis of Capitalism and culture must acknowledge this connection which is present in the relationship between Capitalism and culture. Culture develops under Capitalism, as it does under all societies, but culture is also restricted under Capitalism. In order to liberate culture, to allow it to develop in a liberated and free way, we must liberate culture from Capitalism. In order to do this, we must both understand Capitalism and overcome Capitalism. This essay on culture under Capitalism is a Socialist essay on culture under Capitalism.2

Capitalism and Culture

Capitalism generates economic revolution and social revolution. Indeed, Capitalism brings about a change in the mode of production and the relations of production. This means that Capitalism, by its development, causes a revolution in culture. Indeed, Capitalism brings about a complete change of culture in human societies — often displacing the previous forms of culture which existed beforehand and replacing them with Capitalist culture and Bourgeois culture. This revolution in development brings about a revolution in culture. The reality of the Industrial Revolution of the 19th century, the ultimate form of the transition from Feudalism to Capitalism (1450-1850), brought about a complete revolution in society and culture. Across Europe, by the end of the 19th century, the entire social order had been upturned and replaced with Capitalism and Industrial Capitalism. This revolution in production, and this revolution in social relations, brought about a revolution in culture. Feudal culture was replaced by Capitalist culture. This process of revolution and production, throughout the 19th century and the 20th century, brought about the triumph of Capitalist society and Capitalist culture. The world we live in today is the product of this revolutionary change — in production, in society, and in culture. This revolutionary process, the transition from Feudalism to Capitalism, from 1450 to 1850, was one of the most important revolutionary events of all times. This revolutionary event forms the basis for the current relationship between culture and Capitalism, and the relationship between society and Capitalism. The rise of Capitalism has created the socio-economic conditions for the rise of Socialism. Indeed, the only more revolutionary form of this type of social revolution would be the possible transition from Capitalism to Socialism.

The victory of Capitalism over Feudalism ensured the victory of Capitalist culture over Feudal culture. Across all of the pre-capitalist societies of the world this process has been repeated. Pre-Capitalist culture has been replaced by Capitalist culture in most societies. This destruction of pre-Capitalist society has caused pre-Capitalist culture to be replaced with Capitalist culture.3

Capitalism has used culture to reinforce its economic, political, and social power. This is clear if we look at the overall history of Capitalism — from the fall of Feudalism to the present, from the 1500s to the 2000s. Culture, in modern society, is a tool for the interests of the ruling class. Capitalism, as the dominant economic system, uses culture to reinforce its power and to reinforce its society.

Every major Capitalist Revolution, from the 1500s to the present, has used culture in some form. The English Revolution, the Dutch Revolt, the American Revolution, the French Revolution, the wars of Latin American independence, German unification, and Italian unification, all used culture in order to develop Capitalism itself. Indeed, every major social revolution in history uses culture in some form or another. Capitalist Revolutions promote Capitalist culture. Socialist Revolutions promote Socialist culture. Every social revolution becomes a cultural revolution. The Capitalist Revolutions, of the past and of the present, have used cultural revolution, alongside social revolution.4

The victory of Capitalism, in the 19th century and the 20th century, led to the solidification of Capitalism — both Capitalism itself and Capitalist culture. The cultural impact of this was to shift most of the cultural structures of most societies across the last two centuries. Nearly every culture in the World today has been shaped by Capitalism and Capitalist culture — especially in the West, especially in Europe, and especially in the United States. Even the culture of the ex-Socialist states, after the 1980s, has been shaped, permanently, by the further development of Capitalism.5

The relationship between culture and Capitalism, today, has been shaped by these revolutionary developments. Culture today is shaped by Capitalism. Culture today is mostly the product of Capitalism. This relationship is also shown by the dynamic by which culture exists under Capitalism — the dynamic where culture is turned into a commodity and where culture needs to be profitable in order to be developed. The relationship between culture and Capitalism is a relationship where culture is a commodity and a relationship where Capitalism profits from the sale of culture. This has been the basis of the relationship between culture and Capitalism since the beginning of Capitalism. This has been the relationship between culture and society since the triumph of Capitalism on a global scale. The relationship between culture and Capitalism is the relationship of profit and accumulation. Culture is a commodity under Capitalism.

The development of Capitalism and Capitalist culture needs to be seen in historical terms and in social terms. We cannot understand the current development of culture, under Capitalism, without firmly understanding the historical and social development of Capitalism itself. Culture, in the end, has a history, and its current history, from the 1500s to the present, has mostly been shaped by the history of Capitalism. Not all culture can be reduced to simply the reality of Capitalism, today, otherwise there would be no possibility of Socialism or Socialist culture, today, but it is obvious that the overall development of most culture, today, is shaped by the history of Capitalism. The history of culture, today, is the history of Capitalism. This social reality makes understanding the relationship between culture and Capitalism, between Capitalist culture and Capitalism, much easier from the perspective of the Left, and from the perspective of Socialism. If we can understand the history of Capitalist culture, we might be able to understand the future of Capitalist culture.6

The relationship between culture and Capitalism is similar to the relationship between culture and any class society. Capitalism, like any class society, seeks to use culture for its own aims and its own profit. What differs in the relationship between culture and Capitalism, and culture in other class societies, is primarily in the way in which culture is produced and the ideas which are expressed. Capitalism produces culture through the main mechanisms of Capitalism. Capitalism produces culture to explore and develop the main ideas of Capitalism. This might sound deterministic but in terms of the long-term nature of the relationship between Capitalism and culture this is generally what occurs. Capitalism, even today, is primarily concerned with culture as a means to develop its ideas, to promote its ideas, to propagandise its ideas, and to make profit. This is the overall dynamic of culture under Capitalism. It might differ from place to place and from time to time, in different contexts under Capitalism, but the overall relationship between Capitalism and culture is generally framed by this relationship of ideas, propaganda, and profit. Over two hundred years of cultural history, economic history, and social history, separate the Renaissance from Romanticism — but both were clearly shaped by Capitalism. The overall power of Capitalism is very powerful — it ensures that no form of culture, art, ideas, ideology, or human creativity, produced under it, can escape from its ideas, or its assumptions, or even its process of production. Culture under Capitalism, in one way or another, eventually becomes Capitalist culture. Only the most determined resistance by left-wing art or Socialist art can resist this reality — but even here there are examples of where Capitalism can seize control of those types of culture and use them for its own ends. Picasso and Saramago were both artistic men of the Left — and even they could not escape the reality of their art and their culture becoming part of the reality of Capitalism. In order for culture to escape from Capitalism, culture must break from Capitalism. In order for culture to break from Capitalism, culture must adopt Socialism or become part of Socialism. The work of Picasso has become commercialised — despite his left-wing politics. The work of Saramago is part of international commercial publishing — despite his left-wing politics. Indeed, Socialism must break Capitalism in order for both Socialism and a Socialist culture to emerge. Until then the main relationship between culture and Capitalism will continue to be the same — Capitalism will seek to profit from culture, Capitalism will seek to use culture for its own ideas and its own interests. This means that the power of Capitalism over culture is a powerful one — at least within Capitalist society. As long as Capitalism exists it will continue to dominate and control culture — for its own benefit, and not for the benefit of culture. To break this cycle, we need to break Capitalism and replace it with Socialism. This reality is part of the social struggle of the past and of the present.

The relationship between Capitalist culture and Capitalist society is a dynamic one — both influence and shape each other. Capitalist society, however, ultimately determines Capitalist culture — both in terms of what is produced by Capitalist culture, how it is produced by human labour, and how it is distributed within human society. The political reality of this is that Capitalist culture is ultimately shaped by the economic concerns and the political concerns of Capitalism. This has been the case ever since the emergence of both Capitalist society and Capitalist culture. Capitalist culture, like all culture, cannot escape its social origins or its social roots.

Capitalism will always need a form of culture — both for profit and for propaganda. Capitalism will always need to develop and maintain a form of culture — both as a means of profit-making and as a means of distributing the main ideas of Capitalism. The political effect of this is an interesting one. It ultimately means that Capitalism has changed its culture so greatly that it is difficult to locate what makes Capitalist culture actually capitalist. What makes Capitalist culture actually capitalist is not a particular ideology — like Liberalism or Conservatism — but rather that it is Capitalist because it is a culture which is produced purely for profit and accumulation. Capitalist culture, in the end, is merely and simply the means of making profit on culture. This unites all the various forms of Capitalist culture which have ever existed under Capitalism — and all those forms of Capitalist culture which will ever exist. What unites culture, under Capitalism, from the 1500s to the 2000s, across its history, is the process of profit and accumulation. Culture, under Capitalism, has no other ideas, no other aesthetics, no other hopes, and no other visions, except the vision of making profit and accumulation, from culture itself. This vision of culture, in the end, will destroy itself via its own social contradictions. Capitalist culture, in the end, is a doomed culture, because it is based on these realities of exploitation and oppression. In the end the culture of Capitalism will have to be replaced — hopefully by a Socialist culture and by a Humanist culture.

Capitalist culture, at this point of history, has reached its peak. It is difficult to see how Capitalist culture could develop in the present or in the future. Capitalism will probably linger, on into the future — but this does mean that Capitalism is probably heading for a crisis of its culture, alongside a crisis of its society.7

As Capitalism heads into an uncertain future the growing reality of the crisis of Capitalism becomes more and more obvious. This affects the relationship between Capitalism and culture. The crisis of Capitalism means that culture under Capitalism will always be affected by crisis and by the reality of crisis. Today we can see this around us everywhere. Capitalism is in crisis. The culture of Capitalism is in crisis.

The Crisis of Capitalist Culture

The long development of Capitalist culture has given rise to the reality of Capitalist culture — as it exists today. This culture, in its development over Feudalism, was once very revolutionary and very liberating. In many ways this culture, alongside Capitalism, remains very revolutionary and very liberating — when compared to previous forms of culture in previous forms of class society, such as in Ancient society and in Feudal society. Despite this, from the perspective of today, Capitalism and Capitalist culture is no longer revolutionary or liberating. Capitalism has ceased to be revolutionary — and has become stagnant across the last century, resulting in the stagnation of Capitalism itself, and the stagnation of Capitalist culture.

In this section of the essay, we might briefly describe the crisis of Capitalist culture. Capitalism always produces crisis. Crisis is central to Capitalism. Capitalism has produced crisis in every period and every development of Capitalism, itself, since the 1600s, the 1700s, the 1800s, and the 1900s. Capitalism today, in the 21st century, continues to produce crisis. Most of the time these crises are obvious in economic terms, political terms, and social terms. Capitalism, however, also produces crises of culture — the crisis of Capitalist culture.

Capitalism, Culture, and History

The transition from Feudalism to Capitalism was a long process — from the 1400s to the 1800s. The transition culminated in the Industrial Revolution and the victory of the French Revolution. The long transition from Feudalism to Capitalism generated a cultural revolution and a revolution in culture. Indeed, this revolution took a great deal of time and development — from the Renaissance to Romanticism. The Renaissance, the beginning of modern bourgeois culture, began because of the victory of the Italian City States and their early form of Capitalism. The development of modern British culture took place because of the English bourgeois revolution of the 17th century — the English Revolution of 1640. The development of Romanticism and other bourgeois ideas about culture took place because of the French Revolution of 1789. Everywhere where the transition from Feudalism to Capitalism has occurred, from the 1400s to the present, there has been a cultural revolution and a revolution in culture.

Capitalism emerged from the breakdown of Feudalism. This long process of transition and change, from the 1400s to the 1800s, culminated in a series of great revolutions which brought about the rise of Capitalism and the rise of Industrial Capitalism. The French Revolution and the Industrial Revolution, in particular, led to the victory of Capitalism over Feudalism. In this process there were a series of cultural revolutions which helped to reflect the revolution of Capitalism over Feudalism. The Renaissance, the Enlightenment, Romanticism, and the frequent cultural changes and cultural revolutions in other parts of the world, reflected the importance of culture to the emergence of Capitalism, and to the transition from Feudalism to

Capitalism.

Capitalism changed society — but it also changed culture. This is obvious when we look at the political and social changes which emerged from Capitalism. Capitalism completely destroyed Feudal society and Pre-Capitalist society — across the entire globe. This political result resulted in cultural results. In cultural terms Capitalism produced a culture which was firmly based around the needs of Capitalism and requirements of Capitalism. Capitalism, in cultural terms, produced a culture which replicated and maintained the social relationships generated by Capitalism. Instead of the old social relationships and old cultural relationships of Feudal society, Capitalism produced new social relationships and new cultural relationships. Marx, himself, noted the power of the new social relationships generated by Capitalism — and the new cultural relationships also generated by Capitalism. The power of these new social relationships is well known — as they produced the economic and political reality of Capitalism and of Capitalist production. The power of these new cultural relationships is also well known — as they produced the intellectual structures and intellectual super-structures required to maintain Capitalism. In political terms these new cultural forms of Capitalism were vital — they completely shifted the entire basis of human culture and replaced that basis with an entirely new form of culture: Capitalist culture.

Capitalists and Culture

Capitalists often present themselves as champions of culture. Indeed, one of the key ways in which Capitalists present themselves to the world is via their patronage of the arts. Like the old Feudal lords of medieval Europe or renaissance Europe, the Capitalists of today often spend their wealth in the accumulation of the arts and in the commodification of the arts. Indeed, one of the key aspects of the culture of Capitalism relies heavily on the patronage of Capitalism and the patronage of the capitalist class. When the capitalist class does not spend its capital on accumulation and on commodification it spends its capital on the means of developing its control over the means of production — including the means of cultural production. This power, and this reality, is vital to the cultural power of the Capitalist Class — because, as a class, it can afford to buy culture, sell culture, accumulate culture, and determine the direction of culture. Like the old Feudal lords of the past, the current Capitalists of today dominate contemporary culture — both by determining art and by owning art. The capitalist class accumulates the means of making culture as much as it accumulates the products of culture. The capitalist class accumulates the power of culture as much as it accumulates the results of culture. The capitalist class accumulates profit as much as it accumulates culture and art. In order to understand the power of the capitalist class we also need to understand the cultural power of the capitalist class. Indeed, the capitalist class is vital to the cultural power of Capitalism.

The Capitalists support the development of culture — in order to make profit. This fundamental fact needs to be recognised in terms of the history of Capitalist culture and the politics of Capitalist culture. The capitalist class might seek to develop culture, individually, because of their own, personal, interests, but the social function of culture, for the capitalist class, is profit and the further development of profit. This fact lies at the heart of how Capitalism has produced culture, and popular culture, since the rise of Capitalism itself. We cannot divorce this fact from the systematic nature of culture, under Capitalism, for the capitalist class. All of the economic power and social power devoted to culture, by the capitalist class, exists only because that culture might be able to develop a profit. The whole history of Capitalist culture, and the relationship between Capitalists and culture, reduces itself, in the end, to this format and this reality. It can be seen, again and again, in the history of Capitalism and the history of the capitalist class. This is the same whether we are talking about Capitalist culture in the 16th century or in the 21st century. The power of profit is the vision of culture for Capitalism.

Workers and Culture

Workers can see and feel the reality of culture under Capitalism. Workers, after all, have to live and work in a Capitalist society — and have to struggle to make their own culture under Capitalism. The reality of Capitalist culture shaping and reshaping the culture of the working class is a reality which every worker has experienced — from the day-to-day reality of social struggle to the reality of culture itself changing under Capitalism. The working class has experienced many assaults upon its culture and its values during the long struggles against Capitalism — both in history, in politics, in society, and in culture. Due to the fact that Capitalism is concerned only with profit it does not hesitate to crush and smash the lives of the working class — including the culture of the working class. This fact can be seen both in history and in contemporary society. In history, ever since the emergence of Capitalism, we can see the reality of Capitalism smashing aside working-class culture and working-class values in the pursuit of profit.

The reality of the Industrial Revolution, for example, was heavily based on smashing aside the culture of the early working class — and disciplining them into the order of Capitalism. The solid reality of working-class culture and working-class life has been smashed up, again and again, during the history of Capitalism. The workers have often felt the reality of Capitalism most clearly when their lives and their expectations, their work, and their values, are smashed aside by the economics and politics of Capitalism. This has often caused social struggle and class struggle — as the workers struggle to either maintain their own liberated culture, or to create a new culture. Indeed, some of the most impressive class struggles of history were caused when workers felt the full force of the changes of culture under Capitalism.

The workers have their own culture. The working class has managed to create its own culture, both in historical terms and in political terms. The culture of the working class was made by the working class, as the working class emerged as a modern class in the 1800s and the 1900s. The modern working class, the working class of today, has created a wonderful culture — as shown by the history of working-class culture. Indeed, they have developed their own culture since the beginning of Capitalism and since the emergence of the working class. Today that culture could be the basis for a real and free culture — a Socialist culture. As we develop into the current century hopefully the workers will be able to develop their culture — based on co-operation and solidarity — into a truly global and internationalist culture. Hopefully, the workers will be able to develop their culture into a democratic culture and into a Socialist culture. In order to do this effectively the workers will need to break with Capitalism and establish Socialism. The workers can do this, as shown by history, culture, and politics. The workers can break with Capitalism. The workers can establish a free culture. The workers can establish Socialism.

The workers need to develop their own culture. Indeed, the workers have always developed their own forms of culture — based on solidarity and the struggle for their emancipation from Capitalism. The workers need to develop a culture which stands outside of Capitalism and the culture of Capitalism. Culture, under Capitalism, has nothing to offer the workers — except the basis for the creation of a better and more liberated culture. The workers have the brains and the ability to create culture. Indeed, the workers, as individuals and as a class, have created some of the best culture in the history of humanity. The struggle of the working class for their own culture and their own liberation is the struggle for a better society and a better culture. The workers will make a better culture. They will also make a liberated culture. The workers will abolish the limits of class. They will also abolish the limits of culture. The workers are the basis for a better culture.

The development of working-class politics, in the last two centuries, has given rise to a working-class movement. This movement, the labour movement, and the Socialist movement is capable of achieving the liberation of the working class — the emancipation of the working class. A major part of this process and this struggle for liberation and emancipation, for the working class, is the process of creating a new and better human culture. The working class has this power because it can self-actualise itself as a class — because it has the power of labour and the power of social labour. Social labour, the power of labour, is the basis of social creation. The working class, because it labours, can create new means of production and new forms of production — including new forms of culture. If any class, in existence today, is capable of achieving a new form of society and a new form of culture then that class is the working class. A new form of culture is needed today, given the reality of Capitalism. This new form of culture can only be created by the working class — the only class with the social power necessary to create new forms of culture. Workers and culture are key parts of creating a better humanity. Socialism, as the process of working-class liberation and working-class emancipation, can create a new and better working-class society — and with it a better culture. The social struggle for Socialism is the social struggle for a better culture and society.8

American Culture

American culture, in the United States, is perhaps the best example of Capitalist culture. This is because the United States is the richest and most powerful Capitalist society in existence at this point of history. Before the rise of the United States the most powerful Capitalist society was Great Britain. Today the United States is the most powerful Capitalist society — and as such produces the most powerful form of Capitalist culture. Since 1945, the culture of the United States of America has been the dominant culture in the world — simply by sheer size, economic power, social power, and cultural power. It is a culture which has produced some of the best examples of modern culture – such as the American novel, American film, American music, rock and roll, and Jazz. If we are to understand the development of Capitalist culture, today, we need to understand the development of American culture.9

The United States became the main producer of Capitalist culture in the 20th century. The United States became the main producer of Capitalist culture after 1945. Since the Cold War, the United States has been the main force of Capitalist culture in the World. The sheer power and the sheer scale of American culture makes it the dominant force for Capitalism. The sheer power and the sheer scale of American culture makes it the dominant force for Imperialism. If we truly wish to understand the power of Capitalist culture — in the World today — we must understand the development of American culture and the influence of American culture. The power of Hollywood alone makes American culture important. Indeed, the power of Hollywood and the medium of film was vital to the development of both American culture and Capitalist culture. Without modern film and the modern film industry the ability of American culture to spread across the world would never have developed. The ability of American culture to expand beyond its geographical limits — to conquer the entire world — is an advance of culture which has never happened before in world history. This advance and this power of American culture is important to understand — both in the history of Capitalism and in the struggle for Socialism.10

Capitalist culture in the United States has clearly produced wonderful examples of culture. American film, American literature, and American values are worth developing further. American novels, American films, American music, rock and roll, and Jazz, have all contributed to human culture. The problem is that this great culture is constantly being undermined and commodified by the reality of American Capitalist society. The American values of life, liberty, and the pursuit of happiness, are good values — as values of the revolutionary Enlightenment. The problem is that those values are being corrupted by the nature of American Capitalism and the nature of American Imperialism. The recovery of American culture will require a major social revolution — a major Socialist Revolution.

American society, today, needs social revolution. American society is being destroyed by Capitalism. American society is dominated by Capitalism. There are some great aspects in American culture. Those aspects need to be freed from Capitalism. There is a great deal of American culture which resists Capitalism — or resisted Capitalism. We can think of all the great American left-wing writers of the past two centuries. We can think of all the great left-wing workers in America who formed their own culture. We can think of all the exploited and oppressed minorities in the United States who struggled to make their own culture. This reality of American culture stands outside the Capitalist culture which dominates the United States and the politics of the United States. Any hope for American culture will rest with the ability of the American working class to form their own culture — and to struggle for a better society. Indeed, the very act of resisting Capitalism helps in the development of an alternative culture — a better culture. The United States is not a hopeless cause for the Left. Indeed, if the world is ever to be free from Capitalism, then a great deal will rely on the American working class and the struggle of the American working class. Hopefully, future struggles in the United States will unlock the full potential of American culture — and will help to create a better society: a Socialist society.

The American working class must develop its own culture. If the American workers can develop their own culture, they will not only regain the great ideas of the American Left, they will also gain some of the ideas and agency needed to liberate themselves and their society from Capitalism. The American workers have their own culture — they must take it and develop it. The American working class is part of the international working class – and the international struggle for Socialism. The American working class, as part of the international working class, is crucial for any struggle for Socialism.

Any hope for American culture, today, will come from the hope for Socialism and for Socialist Revolution. Only Socialism and Socialist Revolution will free American culture from the economic chains and the political chains which limit it. American culture needs a Social Revolution in order to free itself from the limits of Capitalist society and from the barbarism of Imperialism.

American society is a revolutionary society — it has had revolutions. The key revolutions of American society remain the American Revolution of 1776 and the American Civil War of 1861-1865. These social revolutions show that America is capable of social revolution. If American culture is to develop today — and develop in human terms — then America requires a new social revolution: a Socialist Revolution.

American culture is some of the most interesting culture in the world. This is because American culture, in the United States, has the power, today, to construct a global culture — a truly global culture. The great expansion of development and production, since the 1800s and since the 1900s, has given American culture the tools to become a global force — while the political development of the United States, since 1945, has made American culture capable of becoming a hegemonic force. There has been no culture, in the history of the planet, with as great a reach and as great a power as American culture today. This means that American culture is interesting, as a social reality of our times. This means that American culture must be understood if we are to understand the United States — both in the present and in the future.11

American culture has a great deal of value. It has produced some great examples of culture. Many of the values and ideas of American culture are compatible with Socialism — particularly the American revolutionary vision of life, liberty, and the pursuit of happiness. If the American people, utilising their own struggles, in all their forms, can unite to achieve a better world for themselves — a Socialist world — they would be able to create an American culture which is free from Capitalism. They might be able to create a new American culture based on the revolutionary legacy of American society and a culture which is capable of building a better United States, for all Americans. The struggle for Socialism in the United States is a key theatre of the struggle for Socialism in general. If we wish to see a Socialist world, we need to establish a Socialist America and a Socialist United States. Hopefully, the American working class, in all their variety and in all their strength, will be able to achieve such a United States — one which will serve their interests and achieve the result of a liberated and changed society in America. Social Revolution, in the United States, is vital to achieving any social progress in the world. Without revolution in the United States there can be no successful revolution in the long term for Socialism — as was shown by the legacy of the struggle in the 20th century.12

The American working class, today, stands at a social crossroads — both as a class and as a working class. The American working class has the power to liberate itself. Either they will achieve a Socialist America, or they will be doomed to the reality of Barbarism in the United States. They, alone, have the power to realise the revolutionary potential of the United States. Hopefully, they will achieve a Socialist America.

The Politics of Capitalist Culture

The politics of Capitalist culture show that culture, under Capitalism, will always be a process of accumulation and profit. While the ideal of culture is the expansion of human knowledge and human liberation the reality of culture, under Capitalism, is one of profit and accumulation. This means that there is always a tension between Capitalism and culture. If we really wish to achieve a better form of culture, we must engage with the politics of Capitalist culture — to understand it, to critique it, and to overthrow it. The politics of Capitalist culture are the politics of using culture for the purpose of profit and accumulation. The politics of Capitalist culture are the politics of using culture to maintain the class system of Capitalism — based on exploitation and oppression. This means that the politics of Capitalist culture will always be framed around this central issue — rather than the liberation of culture. The central contradiction of culture, under Capitalism, is that something which is supposed to liberate humanity is placed within the limited form of profit and accumulation. This reality exists under all forms of Capitalist politics — whether Social Democratic, Liberal, Conservative, or Fascist. The politics of Capitalist culture seek to keep culture under the control of Capitalism. This point is obvious if we look at the political reality of culture under Capitalism — both in history and in politics.13

The Future of Capitalist Culture

The future of Capitalist culture will probably be similar to the past of Capitalist culture. Indeed, the future of Capitalist culture will probably be similar to the present of Capitalist culture. The history and the contemporary reality of Capitalist culture helps to understand the possible future of Capitalist culture — a future of exploitation, oppression, accumulation, and profit. The future of Capitalist culture will be similar to the past and the present of Capitalist culture because no culture can escape the social structures and the social systems which create it. Capitalist culture will always be Capitalist culture. The only way to create a new, better, culture is through the struggle for Socialism. Capitalism has, historically, produced a great deal of great culture — yet it has not been able to create that culture without oppression and without exploitation. The future of Capitalist culture, until Capitalism itself ends, will probably be the same — great culture ruined by the reality of oppression and exploitation. We cannot, completely, predict the future of Capitalism or the future of Capitalist culture. What we can predict is that the future of Capitalism will probably rest on its political reality of exploitation and oppression. So long as Capitalism exists it will be based upon exploitation and oppression. This political reality of Capitalism will always shape the cultural basis of Capitalism — until the day Capitalism is overcome and replaced by Socialism.14

Alternatives

There are alternatives to Capitalist culture. That alternative is Socialism. This alternative must be built if we wish to see a liberated form of culture. Socialism must replace Capitalism if we truly wish to achieve a liberated culture alongside a liberated society. The main point here is that culture under Capitalism will always remain framed by profit — rather than human expression. The other main point here is that culture under Socialism will be framed by human liberation — rather than by profit. The goal of Socialism is human liberation — this includes human culture. The goal of Socialism and culture is to ensure the liberation of culture so that all culture might be enjoyed by all human beings. The liberation of humanity is the liberation of culture. The freedom of humanity is the freedom of culture. Only Socialism will produce the liberty of culture.15 The international working class, by creating Socialism, will produce liberty. The international working class, by creating Socialism, will produce liberty for all.

To conclude this essay, we can briefly outline Capitalist culture and Socialist culture. The key point to make about Capitalist culture and Socialist culture is that Capitalist culture is based on human greed, while Socialist culture is based on human need. Culture, under Capitalism, is simply promoted if it makes a profit. Culture, under Socialism, will be promoted in order to maximise human expression, human liberation, and human feelings. Capitalism only promotes culture in order to profit from it, while Socialism promotes culture in order to ensure real human liberation. This should be clear if we look at the principles and ideas of Capitalism — and the principles and ideas of Socialism. Culture under Socialism is not simply a different vision of culture from culture under Capitalism but a complete transformation of both the social function of culture and the social reality of culture. Capitalism will always see culture as a means to generate profit. Socialism will always see culture as a means of generating human liberation. This simple difference exists because Capitalism is a system of social exploitation and Socialism is not. This simple difference also exists because Capitalism functions in order to maximise its economic power, while Socialism functions in order to place economic power in the hands of the majority. Capitalist culture, in the end, is concerned with profit, exploitation, and accumulation. Socialist culture, in the end, is concerned with humanity, co-operation, and liberation. Socialism will build a better culture – a free culture. It will build a free culture – for all people.

Notes

1. C. Caudwell, Illusion and Reality, (1937)
2. C. Caudwell, Studies in a Dying Culture, (1938)
3. C. Caudwell, Studies in a Dying Culture, (1938)
4. C. Caudwell, Studies in a Dying Culture, (1938)
5. C. Caudwell, Studies in a Dying Culture, (1938)
6. K. Marx, Capital Vol. I, (1867)
7. D. Harvey, Enigma of Capital, (2010)
8. F. Engels, Socialism: Utopian and Scientific, (1880)
9. M. Horkheimer and T. Adorno, Dialectic of Enlightenment, (1947)
10. M. Horkheimer and T. Adorno, Dialectic of Enlightenment, (1947)
11. M. Horkheimer and T. Adorno, Dialectic of Enlightenment, (1947)
12. E.J. Hobsbawm, The Age of Extremes: 1914-1991, (1994)
13. C. Caudwell, Illusion and Reality, (1937)
14. L. Trotsky, Literature and Revolution, (1924)
15. C. Caudwell, Studies in a Dying Culture, (1938)

(2019)

CHAPTER XIV

CULTURE AND SOCIALISM – A MARXIST STUDY

This essay is a study of culture and Socialism. The struggle for human liberation is the struggle for Socialism. Given the reality of Capitalism, and the exploitation caused by Capitalism, the only way to liberate humanity is through Socialism. The struggle for Socialism is the struggle to liberate humanity. This struggle requires a revolutionary struggle — the overthrow of Capitalism by Socialism. This struggle also requires revolutionary ideas — the development of Socialist ideas and Socialist visions. The ideas for a Socialist culture need to be thought about effectively — prior to the struggle for Socialism. It is only when we have an idea about Socialism, and what we wish to achieve in Socialism, that we can really develop the struggle for Socialism. Every theory of Socialism, and every politics of Socialism, needs to engage with the political reality of developing the ideas of Socialism — and the culture of Socialism. Culture, in the broadest sense, is any form of human expression of ideas. For Socialists, culture is an expression of human ideas. It is an expression of humanity that needs to be liberated from Capitalism, in order to fully develop. Capitalism, as exploitation and as oppression, holds back human culture and human freedom. Socialism will liberate the working class and the human race. Socialism will also liberate culture and the means to develop culture. This essay is an attempt to outline some Socialist views about culture and the need to use culture in the struggle for Socialism. Socialism, as a form of human liberation, needs to liberate culture as part of the struggle to liberate humanity. This cultural aspect of Socialism is as important as the social, political, economic, and historical struggle for Socialism. Socialism will liberate culture — and make culture part of the freedom of humanity.

In order to develop a Socialist culture, we need to develop a Socialist view of culture. For Socialists, culture is part of the human experience which emerges from human beings and from human society. Culture is the social expression of human ideas. Culture is an expression of the ideas, principles, values, and concepts of a society. These ideas help to develop society — to push forward its social development and its human development. Culture is that human expression which highlights the ideas and principles of humanity — either as individuals or as societies. The power of culture in human society shows that it is a major force in the development of society. Socialist culture seeks to push culture forward — to utilise culture in the development of a better society, a stateless, classless, equal, democratic, and just society. For Socialism, culture is the human element of human society.1

A Socialist view of culture is to link culture to material society.2 Humanity develops culture in order to express its material reality and its material society.3

A Socialist view of culture is to link culture to historical development. Culture develops, both socially and culturally, through historical development and historical growth.

A Socialist view of culture is to link culture to social struggles and social struggles. Culture develops, socially and economically, through the struggle between classes to express their ideas and their material interests.

The working class, because of its basis in the production of society, is capable of producing a society in which culture is both highly developed and highly free. The working class, through the struggle for Socialism can achieve a society in which human culture and humanity is truly free and truly equal. The Socialist view of culture, in the end, is that culture is an expression of the ability of humanity to develop itself, its interest, and its ideas. Culture is part of the expression of humanity as actually human.4

Socialism

Socialism is the struggle for social control of production by the majority, in the interests of the majority. It is the struggle for human freedom and human emancipation. Socialism, in cultural terms, is the struggle to achieve a real human society — where every person has access to culture, education, and the means and opportunity to develop human culture. Socialism, in those terms, is the struggle to achieve a liberated society. This means that Socialism is a very powerful force for the development of both culture and the democratisation of culture. If we think of Socialism as the struggle for human liberation, which it is, then we can also think of Socialism as the struggle for the liberation of human culture — as culture is a natural product of human beings and human societies. Indeed, every struggle for Socialism has seen an expansion of human culture — and the democratisation of culture to wider parts of human populations. Socialism, at its most basic in terms of principles, is about achieving a society in which the free development of each is the condition of the free development of all. Socialism, at its most basic, is also about achieving a society in which the principle of 'from each according to their ability, to each according to their need' is in operation. These principles, in terms of culture, means the expansion of both culture and the right of societies to develop a truly free culture. Socialism, in cultural terms, is a humanistic culture. Socialism is about economics, politics, society, and history, but it is also about culture — the liberation of culture. All Socialists, around the world, are united by the struggle for the liberation of humanity — particularly the liberation of the working class. The struggle for liberation can be expressed in economic terms and political terms, to achieve a stateless, classless, society — but it also needs to be expressed in cultural terms and in social terms. The struggle for a human culture comes down to the struggle for Socialism. In terms of the liberation of culture, Socialism is one of the more powerful forces in the history of humanity. Socialism will continue to liberate humanity until it achieves the goal of a human society.

It is the argument of this essay that Socialism is crucial to the struggle for a human culture. It is also the argument of this essay that culture is crucial to the struggle for a human Socialism. Socialists work to liberate humanity. To do this Socialism will liberate all men, all women, all groups, and all people. It will liberate all of humanity. To do this Socialism will liberate all from inhumanity.

Socialism will develop culture. Socialism can at least help in the development of a human culture and a humanist culture. Socialism will liberate every man, every woman, every child, every nationality, every race, every sex, every gender, every class, and every person. Socialism will liberate each person and every person. This form of liberation will create a new culture. Such a culture will be developed for every man, woman, child, person, society, race, ethnicity, sex, gender, class, and society. Socialism will develop a free culture — based on the free development of each and the free development of all.

Socialism will liberate culture. Socialism will liberate culture from exploitation and oppression. Socialism will liberate culture from Capitalism. Socialism will liberate culture from Class society.

The modern struggle for Socialism is clearly a struggle to liberate humanity and to overcome the problems facing the World. In many ways the struggle for Socialism can be seen in purely economic terms and political terms, yet Socialism can also be seen in cultural terms — for a better society and a better culture. Clearly Socialism is an economic struggle and a political struggle, to overcome economic and political oppression, but it is also a social struggle to achieve a better society. In the end the struggle for Socialism is holistic — and it includes the struggle for a better culture and a better humanity.

Socialist Culture

In this section of the essay, we might try to outline some basic principles of Socialist culture.

Socialism will create its own society – a liberated society. Socialism will create its own culture. This culture shall be Socialist culture. This type of culture shall take on-board all the social developments of culture from the past, but it will also create its own forms of culture. This type of culture, Socialist culture, shall also liberate all culture — and place it in the hands of all. This type of culture, Socialist culture, will also use culture to achieve the fundamental purpose of all culture — the liberation of humanity. In these terms Socialist culture forms its own form of social revolution — by emancipating society and culture, by emancipating humanity and culture. Instead of placing the basis of culture, as it has often existed, as a process of profit and accumulation, Socialism will open up the basis of culture to all and make that sort of social development of culture the vital process of liberating humanity itself. Socialism will not create a perfect culture — rather it will create a liberated culture. Socialism will create a culture in which every man, every woman, every child, and every person, is free and fully realised. Socialism will create a culture in which the free development of culture shall be based on the free development of each and the free development of all. This type of culture, this approach to culture, has never happened in the history of humanity — a culture in which all of human experience is fully realised in the process of all and in the process of human liberation. This purpose of culture, under Socialism, will be a firmly revolutionary process.

Culture, under Capitalism, is the process of making profit from culture. Culture, under Socialism, is the process of liberating culture in effective terms. Capitalist culture sees culture as a commodity. Socialist culture sees culture as an element of humanity. The social development of society, under Socialism, must be to create a society in which every individual in society is actualised and fully realised. In a sense the goal of Socialism is to create a fully liberated and fully realised humanity. This will be achieved by a social revolution, the transition from Capitalism to Socialism, which will eliminate class society and place the economic, social, political, intellectual, and cultural means of production in the hands of all. Socialism, in cultural terms, means the making of culture and education for all. This applies, equally, to culture. Socialism shall liberate all of human culture because it will liberate every individual and every class in society. The full development of each will become the full development of all, under Socialism, and as a result it will eliminate the economic, social, political, and intellectual restraints which limit humanity and individuals. Socialism will liberate every man, every woman, every child, and every person, and will provide them with the opportunity to contribute to the common production of society and the common production of culture — in a free and equal way. The social power of this form of liberation is immense — it will allow every man, woman, child, and person, to fully realise themselves. This type of social revolution will achieve education and culture for all. This type of social revolution will place education and culture for all in the hands of all. The cultural power of this form of liberation is also immense — as it will allow every man, woman, child, and person, to contribute, fully, to the development of culture.

Culture, under Socialism, can also be seen as a process of enlightenment and development. Socialism will utilise the previous forms of culture, specifically art, music, literature, dance, film, etc., in the further development of culture and in the further appreciation of culture. Indeed, we can think of Socialism as a revolutionary development for culture. Culture, under Socialism, will be revolutionised, but so too will the means to enjoy culture. Socialism will democratise culture and make it so that every person can enjoy all the fruits of culture. Under Socialism, and the process of the full liberation of culture, we shall have a society in which every member of that society can engage with every existing form of culture. We shall open up the benefits of education, development, culture, recreation, and experience, to the reach of all people. Art will no longer be controlled for the process of accumulation but will, instead, become the process of helping to achieve further individual enlightenment and further social enlightenment. Culture, under Socialism, will not be the privilege of a few, but the right of all. Culture will become the basis of a human society — the basis of a real human liberation. This sort of outline might seem utopian — but it is perhaps possible with Socialism, and with a Humanist Socialism.

The fundamental basis of Socialist culture is working-class culture. If any Socialist culture does manage to emerge, both now and in the future, it will be because the working class helped to create that culture and to make that culture. In the end the full historical development of Socialist culture will be based firmly on the working class. The working class, by emancipating itself, will emancipate society, and by emancipating all of society, the working class will emancipate culture. This might sound vague or implausible — but it is how culture is developed, both in social terms and in class terms. The example of the creation of Capitalist Culture, between 1500 and 2000, shows that culture is ultimately the product of a class and of a society. In the future development of Socialist culture that culture will develop because of the working class and because of working-class culture. We cannot really outline all of the elements of Socialist culture, as this would be utopian, rather we need to think of how a future Socialist society will create the basis for a Socialist culture — by liberating the working class, by liberating society, and by liberating culture. In fundamental terms all we can say about Socialist culture is that it is a culture which allows the free development of each and the free development of all. Socialist culture, in the end, will be a liberating culture — one which liberates all of Humanity.

Human liberation, today, can only be achieved by Socialism. Socialism, by liberating all of humanity, by placing the means of production in the hands of the international working class, produces the material basis for human liberation in economic terms, political terms, social terms, scientific terms, technological terms, and cultural terms. This form of liberation is to achieve the free development of each and the free development of all. In terms of culture, Socialism will achieve the goals of the Enlightenment — putting all culture, all art, all learning, into the common reach of each and the common reach of all. Socialism will make culture for all.

Socialist Humanism

Socialism is about the social control of the means of production. In economic terms and political terms this means placing society in the hands of the working class. In social terms this means overcoming class society and abolishing class society. In cultural terms this means developing a new form of culture and a new type of culture. This new form of culture is Socialist Humanism.5

The struggle for Socialism and for humanity, today, is the struggle for Socialist Humanism. The search for a Socialist Humanism is directly connected with the existence of the struggle for Socialism. Indeed, the struggle for both Humanism and for Socialism is impossible, really, without the struggle of both. We cannot have Socialism without Humanism. We cannot have Humanism without Socialism. This point was recognised by Marx himself — but was only really, truly, recognised within Socialist thought during the 1950s and the 1960s, during the time of the New Left, and during the time of the struggle against Stalinism. Our struggle for Socialism, and our struggle for Socialist Humanism must continue on from these previous ideas — as we still have yet to achieve either Socialism or Humanism. Due to the reality of Capitalism, today, with its crises and its destruction of the environment, it is increasingly becoming vital that we establish Socialism and Humanism. Socialist Humanism is not only crucial for the future of humanity, in social terms, it is also vital for the survival of humanity.6

Marx produced an effective way to understand the social realities and the political realities of social development — including Socialism. Marx's method of historical materialism, which studies history and social development by understanding material conditions and material development, can be used to understand Socialism. Historical Materialism shows that history is the result of material conditions, productive forces, social relations, social struggle, class struggle, human agency, and social revolution. Historical Materialism shows that Socialism emerges from social development, economic development, class struggle, social agency, and social revolution. The method of Marx is vital for understanding the connections between Socialism and humanity. For Marx, Socialism was not only a social development for social liberation but part of the social development for human liberation.

Human beings create history. Human beings, as Historical Materialism shows, create history with their labour and with their struggle to achieve a better world. The struggle between classes and the struggle to develop the mode of production, the means of production, and the relations of production, all comes down to the struggle for human self-liberation. The struggle for Socialism, today, is the struggle for human self-emancipation — as shown by Marx's great statement that the emancipation of the working class is the act of the working class itself. Marx understood the social reality of the struggle for human liberation. Marx understood that the human struggle for freedom, self-liberation, and for humanity, leads, in the end, to

Socialism. If we really believe in the universal values of the enlightenment, of democracy, of liberty, of equality, of fraternity, of humanism, of humanity, we end up with the principles of Socialism. A Socialist Humanity, a Socialist Humanism, and a Humanist Socialism, are the results of any real struggle for human liberation. Socialism and Humanity are connected — with one realising the full development of the other. Socialism is not simply a political struggle — it is a social struggle for liberation. Socialism remains, today, the real goal of human development.

The reality of our times demands that we struggle for Socialism. Capitalism is clearly unwilling and unable to solve the key problems of our times. Capitalism, today, is in crisis and is unlikely to solve that crisis in a humane way. The idea that Capitalism can reform itself is a silly idea — as shown by the complete failure of Capitalism to reform since the 1970s, the 1980s, the 1990s, and the 2000s. Despite winning the Cold War, Capitalism has simply plunged humanity into deeper and deeper and deeper crises since the 2000s. Capitalism can offer us no solutions today. Capitalism can only offer us greater and greater and greater crises. The only solution is Socialism.

Humanity has a great amount of potential. Since the emergence of humanity, we have managed to produce a great deal of social advances. We still have the potential to achieve social advances. Socialism, as the social liberation of humanity, by the working class, has the potential to help us, as a species, to achieve our full potential.

The history of Capitalism shows that Capitalism produces the conditions for Socialism. Capitalism produces the economic, social, political, and historical conditions for Socialism. In this sense Capitalism has produced the revolutionary circumstances by which we might achieve a more human society — a Socialist society. The limitation of Capitalism, despite its revolutionary developments, is that it has limited itself to exploitation and oppression. In the world, today, the only way to achieve a more human society, and a more humane society, is via Socialism.

The development of Capitalism might have resulted in huge development for the progress of humanity — indeed, it has resulted in huge development — but that development is finished, today, as a historic force and as a revolutionary force. Capitalism is finished as a truly revolutionary force in world history and world society. It is time for humanity to think about the possibilities of the future — rather than the limits of the past and the present. If we are serious about future human progress, we cannot simply say that

Capitalism, itself, will achieve that progress. Capitalism might have got humanity to its present stage but the idea that Capitalism will last for all of human history is to ignore history itself. Capitalism is merely a simple stage in history. Humanity existed before Capitalism. If we wish for humanity to exist after Capitalism, we must find a better form of society — namely Socialism.

Capitalist society is in crisis today. Capitalist culture is in crisis today. Capitalist society has reached the limits of its historical and economic development. In order for the further liberation of human society to occur we must achieve Socialism. In order to achieve a more developed, enlightened, mature, and free society, we must achieve Socialism. In this sense the struggle for Socialism is the struggle to overcome the limits of Capitalism and the limits of Capitalist society. In terms of achieving the liberation of all of humanity we must achieve Socialism.

If a better world is to emerge from the current crisis of Capitalism we must come up with solutions to the crisis of Capitalism. We must replace Capitalism with Socialism. We cannot simply expect the world to get better. If we expect Capitalism to improve itself, then we will not see any improvement. Indeed, Capitalism, today, is likely to fall into greater and greater crises, again and again, as it struggles to solve its problems. The crisis of Neo-Liberalism and the rise of the Far-Right shows that Capitalism is willing to turn to barbarism in its search to solve its crisis. For Socialists, the current crisis is an opportunity — an opportunity to struggle for Socialism. We cannot, however, simply expect that Capitalism will just turn itself into Socialism, or into something better. We all know that Capitalism would rather turn to barbarism and crisis rather than give up its accumulation, its profits, its exploitation, and its oppression. In the world today, with its crises and class struggles, we can only really solve the problems of the world via the real struggle to achieve Socialism. The struggle for a better world, today, begins and ends with the struggle for Socialism.

Capitalism is retreating from humanity. Indeed, Capitalism is becoming more barbaric. This is clear if we look at the economic crises, political crises, and social crises, which have emerged since the end of the Cold War. While Capitalism won the Cold War, it has only managed to push itself deeper and deeper into crisis. The advance of Capitalism, in the last few decades, has been nothing but an advance into crisis. As a result of its victory Capitalism has simply sought to make more profit, and to conquer larger parts of the globe. The crisis of 2007/2008, the War on Terror, the Afghan War, the Iraq War, the growing climate crisis, the crisis of the environment, the counter-revolution in the Arab world, the crisis in Europe, the rise of the Far-Right, the new Cold War, the threat of nuclear war, and the long wars in the Middle East, show that Capitalism is operating in a period of barbarism. Capitalism is advancing into barbarism.

Stalinism was a betrayal of the humanism of Socialism. Indeed, Stalinism fatally undermined the struggle for Socialism, and a liberated humanity and liberated culture, in the 20th century. The Soviet Union was supposed to be a workers' state — achieving real human liberation. The degeneration of the Soviet Union, into a degenerated workers' state, undermined the struggle for Socialism in the 20th century — and undid the revolutionary struggle of the October Revolution. Today the example of Stalinism shows that a real Socialist culture and a real Socialist society can only emerge from the concrete struggle of ordinary people — which is also the real basis of Socialist Humanism.

The struggle for Socialism, today, is the struggle for Socialist Humanism, for Socialism-Humanism, and for a Socialist Humanity. The only class which can achieve this is the working class. The working class can achieve Socialism because it is the class with the economic, political, and social ability to create Socialism. The working class can achieve Socialist Humanism because it is the class which is the least dehumanised social class, and it is the class with the most humanist social movements. The working class can achieve a Socialist Humanity because it, alone, can create the conditions for a free, equal, and developed, human society in the form of Socialism and Communism. The struggle for human society, human economics, human politics, and human beings, today, is the struggle to find the revolutionary way of achieving this form of Socialism. Socialist Humanism is the only way in which we will achieve both an equal humanity and a liberated humanity. In this sense, Socialism is the most revolutionary social force for humanity.

The struggle for Socialism has to be based on real human liberation. This sort of struggle means that we must seek to use Socialism as the process of liberation itself. Humanity must be made free and liberated, in every aspect of human development. This includes human society and human culture. A key task of any real Socialism must be the liberation of culture, and the expansion of a liberated culture to all. In any real form of Socialism, we must seek to ensure that not only do all human beings have access to culture, but they also have the real basis to contribute to culture. Socialism will liberate both humanity and culture — by making culture part of the very fabric of humanity.

The struggle for Socialism has to be concrete. Socialist Humanism can only exist with the rise of the working class and with the rise of working-class consciousness. Socialist Humanism emerges because of the working class, and it has no other aims than working-class Socialism. The achievement of real human freedom is only really achievable with the achievement of a classless society. This means that Socialist Humanism must be connected to the struggle for Socialism itself. Socialist Humanism is, in the end, part of the human struggle of the working class to achieve Socialism.

The working class has the potential to create Socialism. The working class has the potential to create Socialism because the working class is a class which is the basis for all production in our society. The fact that it is the labour of the working class which creates, develops, shapes, and reproduces society, means that the working class, today, is the only class which can firmly change society and firmly change the world. The working class is capable of Socialism not because it is a moral class or a more ethical class — but because it is based, firmly, in the social level of production necessary to create Socialism. The working class is a revolutionary class because it, alone, has the potential to be truly revolutionary in our society.

The struggle of the working class has created some of the best politics and culture in our society. We should remember the long struggles of the working class — to create our society and the social advances we have enjoyed in the last few centuries. If we wish to see the further progress of humanity, of individuals and of our species, we need to further the struggle of the working class. As Orwell said in 'Nineteen Eighty-Four' (1949): 'If there is hope, it lies in the proles [the working class]'.

The argument of this essay is simple — we need a Socialist Humanity. We need Socialism in order to achieve a human society and a humanist society. We need Socialism in order to achieve a free society. Capitalist society has achieved historical wonders, and wonderful levels of development, but its time as a revolutionary force is finished. Today the only way forward for humanity is the struggle for a new mode of production — for Socialism and for a Socialist society. Socialist Humanism, the ideology of placing human beings at the centre of the struggle for Socialism, remains the best means by which we might achieve both Socialism, a new form of society, and a new form of Socialism.

The argument of this essay is that we need a solution to the inhumanity of Capitalism. The inhumanity of Capitalism is obvious given its real nature and its real development, along with its development in our times. We cannot simply go on, as a human species, believing that Capitalism itself will achieve the progress of humanity. It is time, once again, to put forth the alternatives to Capitalism — the alternative of Socialism. In order to develop such an alternative, we need politics, and we need a sense of political struggle. Our struggle, today, to achieve a liberated humanity must begin and end with building the Socialist alternative to Capitalism — a Humanist Socialism.

Marx's vision of Socialism is a Humanist Socialism. Marx's vision of humanity is the vision of achieving human liberation. Marx's aim is the social liberation of humanity from economic necessity, from economic determinism, and from economic class. Marx's aim is the social liberation of humanity and the individual — so that humanity can achieve the full realisation of humanity and the individual. This is clear in Marx's conception of humanity, from 'The German Ideology' (1845):

> Men can be distinguished from animals by consciousness, by religion or anything else you like. They themselves begin to distinguish themselves from animals as soon as they begin to produce their means of subsistence, a step which is conditioned by their physical organisation. By producing their means of subsistence men are indirectly producing their actual material life...The way in which men produce their means of subsistence depends first of all on the nature of the actual means of subsistence they find in existence and have to reproduce. This mode of production must not be considered simply as being the production of the physical existence of the individuals. Rather it is a definite form of activity of these individuals, a definite form of expressing their life, a definite mode of life on their part. As individuals express their life, so they are. What they are, therefore, coincides with their production, both with what they produce and with how they produce. The nature of individuals thus depends on the material conditions determining their production.7

Marx outlined a theory of humanity — in his theory of species-being (Gattungswesen). Marx's theory of humanity is a theory of human liberation — in the form of Socialism. Marx believed that humanity is capable of labour and of creativity. Indeed, humanity is unique in this sense, in its ability to both labour and to create. Marx's theory of humanity, as outlined in 'The Economic and Philosophical Manuscripts of 1844' (1844) is clear on this point — humans are capable of creative production and creative labour:

> Man is directly a natural being. As a natural being and as a living natural being he is on the one hand endowed with natural powers, vital powers — he is an active natural being. These forces exist in him as tendencies and abilities — as instincts. On the other hand, as a natural, corporeal, sensuous objective being he is a suffering, conditioned and limited creature, like animals and plants. That is to say, the objects of his instincts exist outside him, as objects independent of him; yet these objects are objects that he needs — essential objects, indispensable to the manifestation and confirmation of his essential powers.8

Marx's theory of humanity is the theory of human liberation through labour, culture, co-operation, and social revolution. This point is crucial if we are to understand Marx — and Marx's theory of Socialism. Marx saw Socialism as the process of the liberation of real humanity. This is clear in 'The Economic and Philosophical Manuscripts of 1844' (1844):

> Objective man — true, because real man — as the outcome of man's own labour. The real, active orientation of man to himself as a species-being, or his manifestation as a real species-being (i.e., as a human being), is only possible if he really brings out all his species-powers — something which in turn is only possible through the cooperative action of all of mankind, only as the result of history — and treats these powers as objects: and this, to begin with, is again only possible in the form of estrangement.9

Marx conceived of human history as the development of the means of achieving human liberation — from economic development to social development, from class society to a classless society. Marx's conception of human history is the conception that human history is the development of economic development, social development, class struggle, and social revolution, for the purposes of achieving real human liberation. For Marx, humanity is central to his conception of history. This is also clear in Marx's conception of historical materialism, in 'The German Ideology' (1845):

> The first premise of all human history is, of course, the existence of living human individuals. Thus, the first fact to be established is the physical organisation of these individuals and their consequent relation to the rest of nature. Of course, we cannot here go either into the actual physical nature of man, or into the natural conditions in which man finds himself — geological, hydrographical, climatic and so on. The writing of history must always set out from these natural bases and their modification in the course of history

through the action of men.10

Marx outlined his theory of history as the theory of historical materialism. This theory suggests that human history is based on material conditions, productive forces, social relations, social struggle, class struggle, human agency, and social revolution. This theory of history sees culture, ideology, ideas, and art, as powerful social forces, which are produced by societies, as part of the social superstructure of society. Marx showed the connection between culture, society, revolution, and history, in 'Preface to a Contribution to the Critique of Political Economy' (1859):

> In the social production of their existence, men inevitably enter into definite relations, which are independent of their will, namely relations of production appropriate to a given stage in the development of their material forces of production. The totality of these relations of production constitutes the economic structure of society, the real foundation, on which arises a legal and political superstructure and to which correspond definite forms of social consciousness. The mode of production of material life conditions the general process of social, political and intellectual life. It is not the consciousness of men that determines their existence, but their social existence that determines their consciousness. At a certain stage of development, the material productive forces of society come into conflict with the existing relations of production or — this merely expresses the same thing in legal terms — with the property relations within the framework of which they have operated hitherto. From forms of development of the productive forces these relations turn into their fetters. Then begins an era of social revolution. The changes in the economic foundation lead sooner or later to the transformation of the whole immense superstructure.11

Marx once wrote about the importance of humanism and humanity in the creation of a better world. His entire vision of Socialism and of Communism is based on the idea that humanity can achieve better forms of development and better forms of society. Marx believed in Socialism as the basis for achieving the end of exploitation, oppression, and alienation. Marx believed that the abolition of class would eliminate the social basis for the inhumanity of humans against humans. Marx also believed that Communism, as the liberation of each and the liberation of all, would eliminate the basis of human alienation — especially human alienation from our species and our species-being — allowing humanity to revolutionise its ability to create and produce. Marx's entire vision of Socialism and Communism is the basis of achieving the very real liberation of all people — so that all people might develop as free human beings. Marx's concept of species-being (Gattungswesen) is that humans, naturally, are creative — and should be creative. For Marx, the struggle for a higher level of society brings about the struggle for a better form of humanity. Marx's conception of humanity was firmly based on the need to liberate humanity — in order for humanity to really achieve its potential. This is also clear in Marx's writing, from 'The German Ideology' (1845):

> Man is a species-being, not only because he practically and theoretically makes the species — both his own and those of other things — his object, but also — and this is simply another way of saying the same thing — because he looks upon himself as the present, living species, because he looks upon himself as a universal and therefore free being.12

Marx's vision of humanity is connected to his vision of politics — the process of human liberation and human emancipation via Socialism. Marx's entire vision of Socialism is the vision of achieving a society based on real human liberation. Marx's goal is always the goal of the liberation of each and the liberation of all. Marx outlined this, firmly, in 'The Communist Manifesto' (1848):

> The first step in the revolution by the working class is to raise the proletariat to the position of ruling class to win the battle of democracy. … If the proletariat during its contest with the bourgeoisie is compelled, by the force of circumstances, to organise itself as a class, if, by means of a revolution, it makes itself the ruling class, and, as such, sweeps away by force the old conditions of production, then it will, along with these conditions, have swept away the conditions for the existence of class antagonisms and of classes generally, and will thereby have abolished its own supremacy as a class. In place of the old bourgeois society, with its classes and class antagonisms, we shall have an association, in which the free development of each is the condition for the free development of all.13

Marx believed in a liberated humanity. This is shown by his great statement — the free development of each and the free development of all. This was central to his vision of Socialism. Indeed, Marx's Socialism is the idea and the practice of the liberation of humanity from exploitation, oppression, and alienation. In terms of alienation, we can firmly see the reality of class society generating the economic and social basis for alienation. If we wish to have a liberated society, a liberated humanity, one which is free from alienation, and free to expand itself and its ideas, then we must abolish the root causes of alienation — namely the class system. Marx expressed this vision for Socialism in the 'Economic and Philosophical Manuscripts of 1844' (1844):

> Communism, as fully developed naturalism, equals humanism, and as fully developed humanism equals naturalism; it is the genuine resolution of the conflict between man and nature and between man and man — the true resolution of the strife between existence and essence, between objectification and self-confirmation, between freedom and necessity, between the individual and the species. Communism is the riddle of history solved, and it knows itself to be this solution.14

Marx's vision of a liberated humanity is the vision of a liberated individual. Marx believed, completely, that the victory of Socialism would be the victory of a co-operative society — a society made up of free individuals working in free association, based on the principle of the free development of each and the free development of all. Such a vision is, fundamentally, about the liberation of both individuals and society. Socialism, in the end, is the victory of human liberation. Marx made this clear in 'Critique of the Gotha Programme' (1875):

> In a higher phase of communist society, after the enslaving subordination of the individual to the division of labour, and therewith also the antithesis between mental and physical labour, has vanished; after labour has become not only a means of life but life's prime want; after the productive forces have also increased with the all-around development of the individual, and all the springs of co-operative wealth flow more abundantly — only then can the narrow horizon of bourgeois right be crossed in its entirety and society inscribe on its banners: From each according to his ability, to each according to his needs.15

Marx believed in the liberation of culture — to make culture part of the development of each and the development of all. By abolishing Capitalist society, and class society, we shall achieve a society in which all people will have the means to develop their own vision of culture. By abolishing the economic basis for exploitation and oppression we shall have the economic basis for establishing co-operation and solidarity. Marx's vision of Socialism is the vision of a liberated society, as outlined in 'The German Ideology' (1845):

> In communist society, where nobody has one exclusive sphere of activity but each can become accomplished in any branch he wishes, society regulates the general production and thus makes it possible for me to do one thing today and another tomorrow, to hunt in the morning, fish in the afternoon, rear cattle in the evening, criticise after dinner, just as I have a mind, without ever becoming hunter, fisherman, herdsman or critic.16

Socialism and humanity are intrinsically connected. There is no way to understand either humanity, or Socialism, without understanding the connection between the two. Indeed, Socialism is humanity, and humanity is Socialism. To try to separate the two is impossible in any social reality, political reality, or historical reality. Marx understood this point in his vision of Socialism itself— as a real process of human liberation. This is also clear in 'The German Ideology' (1845):

> Communism is for us not a state of affairs which is to be established, an ideal to which reality [will] have to adjust itself. We call communism the real movement which abolishes the present state of things. The conditions of this movement result from the premises now in existence.17

Culture and Crisis

Society, today, is in the middle of a major crisis. Indeed, this crisis is the reality of trying to achieve Socialism under Capitalism. Capitalism is in crisis — not only with its own crisis but with the crisis of a new Socialist society struggling to emerge from Capitalism. Capitalism will always throw society into crisis — as it throws humanity into crisis. Our society, today, is marred by the reality of exploitation, oppression, and crisis. The struggle, today, in the humanity of Socialism, is to build a new humanity and a new Socialism — a liberated humanity, a liberated Socialism. The struggle, today, is to build a Socialist humanity, a humanist Socialism, a Socialist Humanism, and a Socialist Humanity. This is the task of our times — which is the only way to revolutionise our society and our Socialism.

Politics, today, is in crisis. The only humane way to solve this crisis is for the Left to build Socialism — a Humanist Socialism. If we succeed, we might yet build a better world — one based on human emancipation and human freedom. If we fail then the alternative is the continuation of the crisis, the barbarism of conflict, the barbarism of war, the barbarism of environmental collapse, the barbarism of Capitalism, and the barbarism of Fascism. Our struggle is to achieve the former — to achieve Socialism and a Socialist Humanism.

Politics is the struggle of classes. The fundamental politics, of our time, is the struggle between the capitalist class and the working class. The capitalist class seeks to maintain the barbarism of Capitalism. The working class seeks to achieve the humanity of Socialism. The struggle of our times is the struggle to, at last, achieve the humanity of Socialism.

Liberation

Socialism shall liberate culture. Socialism, in cultural terms, is simply the process of liberating both humanity and culture — and of placing culture in the hands of all.

Socialism, in creating a society based on the liberation of each and the liberation of all, shall create a society in which culture exists in the hands of each and in the hands of all.

Socialism will achieve a liberation of culture — because it will eliminate the economic, social, political, and intellectual constraints which constrain culture and society itself.

Socialism, as liberation, will be both the liberation of society and the liberation of culture. In many ways the liberation of humanity relies on both forms of liberation. If we can liberate humanity from the economic, social, political, and intellectual limits of class society we might liberate humanity from the limits of culture itself — producing the means for a common culture and a human culture.

We can only achieve Socialism via revolution. A reformist road to Socialism might achieve reforms and improvements, for humanity, for society, and for culture, but the real basis of human liberation, in achieving Socialism, will be achieved by the revolutionary struggle for Socialism. Revolution will bring about Socialism — and Socialism will bring about real human liberation.

The historical and political development of Socialism has generally led to the liberation and development of culture. When the working class is able to liberate itself, it usually leads to the liberation of culture. When the working class liberates itself, it can lead to the liberation of all society.

The goal of Socialism is to achieve human liberation. One of the key aspects of this goal is to achieve the full liberation of culture. If we can achieve a liberated society, we might be able to achieve a liberated culture. The power of this human liberation will result in the power of a liberated culture. This is the cultural power of Socialism — it will result in our ability to create culture and to enjoy culture on a truly human scale. We will use culture to build Socialism. We will use Socialism to build culture. The full impact of Socialism will be the fact that all will be able to enjoy this new culture — in a free and determined way. The full result of Socialism is not only the liberation of humanity, but the liberation of culture. We will build a better culture. We will build Socialism.

Notes

1. C. Caudwell, Illusion and Reality, (1937)
2. C. Caudwell, Studies in a Dying Culture, (1938)
3. K. Marx, The German Ideology, (1845)
4. E.P. Thompson, Socialist Humanism, (1957)
5. E.P. Thompson, Socialist Humanism, (1957)
6. E.P. Thompson, Socialist Humanism, (1957)
7. K. Marx, The German Ideology, (1845)
8. K. Marx, The Economic and Philosophical Manuscripts of 1844, (1844)
9. K. Marx, The Economic and Philosophical Manuscripts of 1844, (1844)
10. K. Marx, The German Ideology, (1845)
11. K. Marx, Preface to a Contribution to the Critique of Political Economy, (1859)
12. K. Marx, The German Ideology, (1845)
13. K. Marx and F. Engels, The Communist Manifesto, (1848)
14. K. Marx, The Economic and Philosophical Manuscripts of 1844, (1844)
15. K. Marx, Critique of the Gotha Programme, (1875)
16. K. Marx, The German Ideology, (1845)
17. K. Marx, The German Ideology, (1845)

(2019)

CHAPTER XV

CULTURE AND REVOLUTION

This short essay is a study of culture and revolution. Culture is a key part of revolution and revolutionary struggle. Culture helps to develop the ideas and the ideals which often shape revolution and revolutionary struggle. Every social revolution in history has had cultural ideas and cultural revolutions. The Capitalist revolutions, of the past, produced advances in Capitalist culture. The Socialist revolutions, of the past, produced advances in Socialist culture. Future Socialist revolutions will produce further advances in culture.

Most revolutions have produced cultural revolutions. This is a natural result of social revolution achieving changes in society, which leads to changes in society and in culture. The history of society is the history of social revolution.1

Cultural revolutions can be part of social revolutions. This is clear if we look at both the revolutions of the past and the revolutions of today. Cultural revolutions are a powerful part of any social revolution.

Social revolutions, in history, have produced cultural revolutions. The emergence of humanity, through human evolution, produced a cultural revolution. The rise of class society, after the neolithic revolution and after the urban revolution, produced a cultural revolution. The rise of ancient society produced a cultural revolution. The rise of Feudal society produced a cultural revolution. The rise of Capitalist society produced a cultural revolution. The rise of Socialist society will produce a cultural revolution.2

Political revolutions, in history, have produced cultural revolutions. The English Revolution produced a cultural revolution. The American Revolution produced a cultural revolution. The French Revolution produced a cultural revolution. The Russian Revolution produced a cultural revolution. The Revolutions of the 1960s produced a cultural revolution. Every political revolution, including future Socialist revolutions, will produce social revolution and cultural revolution.3

Culture also has its own forms of revolution — which emerge from social revolutions and political revolutions. The Renaissance, the Reformation, the Enlightenment, the Industrial Revolution, the French Revolution, the October Revolution, and the numerous other social/cultural revolutions of the last two centuries, all produced social revolution and cultural revolution.4

Culture is powerful. Culture, however, cannot generate a revolution. Culture, as a product of the superstructure of a society, can only inform revolutions which are already developing due to social struggle and due to social conflicts. Culture can make revolution, but culture cannot make revolution by itself or for itself. Cultural forms of revolution always need to be united with social revolutions and political revolutions — in order to become effective revolutions.

Any historian of revolution can show that culture alone, even a revolutionary culture, cannot produce a revolution. Revolutions emerge for economic reasons, social reasons, and political reasons — not for cultural reasons.5

This fact of history and politics shapes our struggle, today, for revolution and for Socialist revolution. If the Socialist revolution is to be successful, we need a revolutionary culture — but that cannot be the basis of the revolution. The revolution must be based on the social struggle and the political struggle for Revolution.

Capitalist society, today, has a great deal of revolutionary potential. We do not need to base the struggle for revolution, today, in cultural terms. Instead, we can easily base it on the economic reality that Capitalism is in crisis and the political reality that Capitalism is in crisis. This argument is a stronger argument about the need for revolution than any argument drawn from culture or cultural problems. Indeed, the only way to solve culture or cultural problems is through revolution — through social revolution, political revolution, economic revolution, and Socialist revolution.6

Culture, alone, cannot change society. This does not mean that culture is irrelevant to revolution. It merely means that culture alone cannot make revolution. Any successful revolution will bring about a revolution in society and a revolution in culture — but that is a by-product of the revolution itself, not the basis of the revolution itself. Marx understood this when he defined the revolution of the working class, the revolution to achieve Socialism, as a social revolution.

If we look at the history of revolution, we can see that revolutions do not begin in cultural terms. They begin in social terms. The English Revolution of 1640, the American Revolution of 1776, the French Revolution of 1789, the Russian Revolution of 1917, the Chinese Revolution of 1949, and all the other great social revolutions of history, began as social revolutions — not as cultural revolutions. Indeed, it is politically impossible to make a cultural revolution without first making a social revolution — as shown by the history, and by the politics, of previous social revolution.7

If we look at the history of revolutions, we can see that revolutions bring about social results, economic results, and political results before they bring about cultural results. It is only when changing the base of society — the mode of production — and the superstructure of society, that we can see changes in the culture of society. The history of revolution is the history of economic revolution, social revolution, and political revolution, leading to social change and cultural revolution.8

Culture is still important to revolution. It is certainly important in both the short-term results and the long-term results of revolution. We cannot, however, base any revolution which might actually succeed purely on cultural change and cultural revolution. A change in the base of society must come before there is a change in the superstructure of society. All great social revolutions follow this pattern of development. All great social revolutions follow this pattern of struggle.

People on the Left today can see the need for revolution. The sort of revolution which is needed is a social revolution — a revolution which changes society by overthrowing one economic system and replacing it with another, a revolution which overthrows Capitalism and replaces it with Socialism. Cultural revolution can emerge from this type of social revolution — but cultural revolution cannot generate this type of social revolution. Social revolution, today, is the only way to achieve Socialism.

Revolutions in society are inevitable. Revolutions have already happened in the history of society and revolutions will always occur in the history of society. This inevitability means that preparing for social revolution requires having a detailed understanding of the development of society and of the historical development of society. Culture can be part of this revolution — but it is not the basis of the revolution itself.

The revolution to achieve Socialism will probably follow a similar pattern as earlier social revolutions. The revolution to achieve Socialism will emerge from economic conditions, political conditions, social conditions, and historical conditions — rather than cultural conditions. The revolution to achieve Socialism will be the greatest social revolution in the history of humanity. It will free society and it will free culture. The Socialist revolution will mark the end of class society and will bring about the beginning of a liberated human society.

It is the fear of revolution which causes counter-revolution. This fear will not prevent revolution forever. Revolution will come and revolution will be victorious. No counter-revolution can hold back history forever — just as the French Kings and the Russian Tsars learned. History moves forward thanks to Revolution. History will move forward, eventually, towards Socialism.9

Socialist culture is an international culture. If we ever hope to heal the divisions of the world today, then Socialism will be vital. The divisions of the world created by the end of the Cold War can still be overcome — and Socialism will be vital in achieving that. Yet we cannot rely on culture and cultural revolution alone to achieve this. Instead, we must struggle to achieve economic revolution, political revolution, and social revolution. It is on this basis that Socialist Revolution will be made — and it is on this basis that humanity will make Socialism.10

Achieving a Socialist culture will require achieving a Socialist society. If we are to ever achieve Socialism, we cannot do it simply through cultural revolution or through a revolution of culture. In order to achieve Socialism, we need economic revolution, political revolution, social revolution — a revolution which changes society at its base and its superstructure. Cultural forms of revolution can help in this regard but the only way to actually achieve Socialism is to achieve an actual Socialist revolution. Socialism will emerge via revolution — but that revolution needs to be a social revolution. The struggle for Socialism is the revolutionary struggle for Socialism.11

The idea that culture itself can change society is a flawed idea. It has no basis in Socialist thinking or in Marxist thinking. Indeed, the only people who seem to make this argument exist on the Right — and in the flawed thinking of the Right. Revolution occurs, in the end, because of social revolution.12 It is social revolution which, ultimately, brings about social change. It is this dynamic, of social revolution creating cultural and social change, which must inform any real understanding of achieving a better world today.

Notes

1. K. Marx, Speech at Anniversary of the People's Paper, (1856)
2. R. Williams, Culture and Society, (1958)
3. R. Williams, Culture and Society, (1958)
4. R. Williams, The Long Revolution, (1961)
5. R. Williams, The Long Revolution, (1961)
6. K. Marx, Preface to a Contribution to the Critique of Political Economy, (1859)
7. K. Marx, Preface to a Contribution to the Critique of Political Economy, (1859)
8. K. Marx and F. Engels, The Communist Manifesto, (1848)
9. K. Marx, Preface to a Contribution to the Critique of Political Economy, (1859)
10. L. Trotsky, Permanent Revolution, (1930)
11. L. Trotsky, Literature and Revolution, (1924)
12. V. G. Childe, Man Makes Himself, (1936)

(2016)

CHAPTER XVI

TOWARDS A SOCIALIST CULTURE

This short essay is a study of the struggle for a Socialist culture. The world today is faced with many key crises. These crises are the crisis of Neo-Liberalism, the crisis of Capitalism, the crisis of Capitalist society, the crisis of Imperialism, the crisis of war, the crisis of nuclear weapons, the threat of Fascism, and the crisis of the environment. These are all social crises. There are also other crises — specifically the crisis of culture. Indeed, all of these problems point to a crisis of Capitalist society — and the need for Socialism.

It is clear, today, that Capitalism is incapable of solving these crises and these problems. Indeed, it is also clear that Capitalism has created these problems and is furthering these problems. The reality of these crises means that an alternative to Capitalism must be developed — that alternative is Socialism.

Capitalism needs to be confronted by Socialism. The crises of Capitalism need to be overcome by Socialism. Capitalism needs to be overthrown by Socialism. The reality of Capitalism needs to be replaced by Socialism. Capitalism needs to be understood by Socialism. The culture of Capitalism needs to be replaced by the culture of Socialism.

Socialism is a society based on the social control of the means of production, a society based on equality and co-operation, a society based on the working class. Socialism is a society based on the principle of 'from each according to their ability, to each according to their need', as outlined by Marx and others. It is only Socialism which can solve the crises of the world today — and overcome the reality of Capitalism.

The problems of Capitalist society mean that Capitalism is incapable of producing a genuinely humane society. The fact that Capitalism is built on oppression and exploitation shows that Capitalism cannot produce a human society for all humans. Only Socialism, built on equality and co-operation, against hierarchy and exploitation, can overcome the realities of Capitalism.

This political fact, and this economic fact, has been clear since the 1800s — since the Industrial Revolution. This social fact, and political fact, has been clear since the 1800s — since the emergence of the struggle for Socialism.1

Human culture can be a tool in the struggle against Capitalism. Culture can be used to develop the struggle for Socialism — here and today. Culture can be used to develop the ideas of Socialism and to apply the ideas of Socialism. Culture can be used to ensure that Socialism will build a genuinely human and humane society. This short essay is an attempt to outline some ideas towards a Socialist culture — in order to develop the ideas of Socialism and the struggle for Socialism. Of course, a Socialist culture cannot be developed, fully, until a Socialist society has been built, but thinking about the ideas and principles of a Socialist culture can help to develop further the ideas and principles of Socialism. If we wish to build a truly human society — a humanistic Socialism — we must first have some ideas about the means of thinking about that society. The struggle for Socialism is the struggle for the ideas of Socialism. The struggle for Socialism is the struggle for the culture of Socialism.

Socialism is the basis of building a better society and a better culture. Socialism will build the basic forces and basic tools needed to create a better culture — a culture in which all of humanity can express itself and develop itself. Socialism can do this because it bases its production of culture on the principle of human need — not the principle of profit. Socialism can liberate culture in a way that Capitalism cannot. Capitalism might develop culture and profit from culture, but Capitalism cannot truly liberate culture or build a fully human culture. Only Socialism can build the basis of a human culture — one which develops all culture. Socialism can develop culture because it is based on the principle: 'the free development of each is the condition for the free development of all'.2

Capitalism, in the past two centuries, has developed society and culture. Indeed, it has created many tools for the production of culture — from the printing press to film. What Capitalism has not done, however, is liberate the means of production necessary for the production of culture. Instead, Capitalism has always tried to profit from the exploitation of culture — both old cultures and new cultures. Capitalism does not care about culture — it cares about the profit of culture. This reality means that Capitalism cannot truly liberate culture. Only Socialism can truly liberate culture and make culture the expression of the whole of humanity.

The working class is the basis of Socialism. It is the working class, by their organisation and their struggle, which will create Socialism and create the basis for a Socialist culture. By liberating themselves and by liberating society, the working class will liberate humanity and will liberate culture.

The working class can create both Socialism — and Socialist culture. Working-class culture is the basis of Socialist culture. The working class, who will build Socialism, have already developed their own culture. Indeed, some of the best examples of culture to have emerged since the 19th century have emerged either from the working class or because of the working class. The working class has contributed to the development of human culture in every area of culture — in every type of culture. The working class is the basis by which most culture is produced today — even in the form of providing the basic tools by which culture is produced. Every film, every book, every novel, every poem, every piece of artistic work, at some level or another, relies on the working class — either to produce it, to create it, or to develop the forces of production which create that culture. The working class is the basis of all culture today. Working-class culture is a basis from which to build a Socialist culture.

The power of culture is evident in our society. Culture can emerge from the economic base of society to become a key part of the ideological superstructure of society. This means that while culture is determined by the economic base of society it can also shape that economic base. The intellectual power and the ideological power of culture in the shaping of society is vital to understand — both in society today and in any real struggle for a liberated society. Culture is part of the superstructure of society — it helps to shape society. A Capitalist society creates a Capitalist culture. A Socialist society will create a Socialist culture.3

Culture will be vital for any struggle for a better society and a better world. The workers of the world, the exploited of the world, the oppressed of the world, need to develop both their struggle and their culture, in order to produce a better world. Culture, alongside the struggle for Socialism, can help in this struggle. The workers of the world need to unite around their common interests and use this to build a common culture and a common society. It is only on this basis that a better society can be built. If we are ever to move towards a Socialist World we will need to move towards a Socialist culture.

Socialism is international and internationalist. The vision of Socialism, in cultural terms, is to achieve a society where all workers, peoples, nations, ethnicities, groups, creeds, nationalities, religions, languages, races, genders, sexes, and all exploited and oppressed peoples, are free to develop their freedom and their culture. In social terms, Socialism is simply the achievement of human freedom. Indeed, the struggle for Socialism is the struggle for liberation, for all peoples, without distinction, and with freedom for all. We must achieve a society which is fully committed to the liberation of each and the liberation of all. The struggle for Socialism is the struggle to free all — so that each is free, and all are free. Socialism, in cultural terms, is the process of the liberation of all parts of the world, and all peoples in the world, so that all peoples can enjoy all of culture. The struggle for Socialism, as Marx said, is a global struggle — 'the emancipation of labour is neither a local nor a national, but a social problem, embracing all countries'. The struggle of Socialism is to achieve emancipation for all and liberation for all. The struggle for Socialism, in this form, is the struggle for a liberated humanity.

The hope of Socialism is the hope of the world. This basic idea has been a clear idea since the 19th century — since the Industrial Revolution created the political reality that Socialism is possible. The struggle for Socialism has been long and hard — indeed, it has yet to be fully completed. If there is any hope for the future of humanity — for a good future — that hope is Socialism.

The hope of Socialism is also the hope for a liberated humanity. Capitalism cannot produce a liberated humanity — because it is built on exploitation and oppression. Socialism can produce a liberated humanity — because it abolishes exploitation and oppression and replaces it with co-operation and equality. Socialism, in the end, must be a society based on human dignity, human rights, human freedom, and humanity itself. This is why Socialism must be Humanist and why Humanism must be Socialist. By abolishing class, Socialism will build a better society — a society for all of humanity.

Socialism is the real basis of the real freedom of humanity. To fight for Socialism is to fight for humanity. To fight for Socialism is to fight against Totalitarianism and for Democratic Socialism.4

The only way to achieve a truly free society is to achieve a society where all peoples and all societies have the means to develop their own culture and their own development — in the process of self-determination. The struggle for a Socialist culture is not the struggle to abolish any specific culture or any national culture. The struggle for a Socialist culture is the struggle to achieve a world where all cultures, in all forms, are free to develop themselves — for the process of the liberation of all societies and all culture. Only this process will achieve a free society. Humanity must build a free society.

Notes

1. R. Williams, Culture and Society, (1958)
2. K. Marx and F. Engels, The Communist Manifesto, (1848)
3. K. Marx and F. Engels, The Communist Manifesto, (1848)
4. G. Orwell, Why I Write, (1946).

(2016)

BIBLIOGRAPHY

Anderson Perry and Blackburn Robin (ed.), Towards Socialism, (London: New Left Books, 1966).

Anderson Perry, 'Origins of the Present Crisis', (1964) New Left Review, I/23, January-February, 1964.

Anderson Perry, Considerations on Western Marxism, (London: Verso, 1976).

Anderson Perry, Arguments within English Marxism, (London: Verso, 1980).

Anderson Perry, In the Tracks of Historical Materialism, (London: Verso, 1983).

Anderson Perry, 'Two Revolutions', (2010), New Left Review 61, January/February, 2010.

Benjamin Walter, 'On the Concept of History', (1940), in Howard Eiland and Michael W. Jennings (ed.), Walter Benjamin: Selected Writings, 4: 1938–1940, (Cambridge, Massachusetts, Harvard University Press, 2006).

Benjamin Walter, The Author as Producer, (1970) in New Left Review 1/62, July-August 1970.

Berman Marshall, All That Is Solid Melts Into Air, (London: Verso, 1983).

Caudwell Christopher, Illusion and Reality: A Study of the Sources of Poetry, (New York: International Publishers, 1937).

Caudwell Christopher, Studies in a Dying Culture, (London: Bodley Head, 1938).

Caudwell Christopher, Further Studies in a Dying Culture (London: Lawrence and Wishart, 1949).

Childe V.G., Man Makes Himself, (London: Watts and Co, 1936).

Childe V.G., What Happened in History, (Harmondsworth, Penguin Books, 1942).

Draper Hal, 'The Two Souls of Socialism', (1963) in New Politics 5, no.1, Winter 1966, pp.57-84.

Dunayevskaya Raya, "Marx's Humanism Today", in Erich Fromm (ed.), Socialist Humanism, (New York: Doubleday 1965).

Eagleton Terry, Marxism and Literary Criticism, (Berkeley: University of California Press, 1976).

Engels Friedrich, Socialism: Utopian and Scientific, (1880), (London by Swan Sonnenschein and Co, 1892).
Fischer Mark, Capitalist Realism, (London, Zero Books, 2009).
Fromm Erich, Marx's Concept of Man, (New York: Frederick Ungar Publishing Co, 1961).
Gorky Maxim, Untimely Thoughts, (1917-1918), (New Haven: Yale University Press, 1995).
Gramsci Antonino, Selections from the Prison Notebooks (London: Lawrence and Wishart 1971).
Harvey David, A Short History of Neo-Liberalism, (Oxford: Oxford University Press, 2005).
Harvey David, The Enigma of Capital and the Crises of Capitalism, (Oxford: Oxford University Press, 2010).
Hobsbawm Eric, The Age of Revolution: 1789-1848, (London: Weidenfeld and Nicolson, 1962).
Hobsbawm Eric, The Age of Extremes: 1914-1991, (London: Michael Joseph, 1994).
Horkheimer Max and Theodore Adorno, Dialectic of Enlightenment, (New York: Social Science Association, 1944/1947).
James C.L.R., World Revolution: 1917-1936, (London, Secker and Warburg, 1937).
James C.L.R., 'Dialectical Materialism and the Fate of Humanity', (1947), in Anna Grimshaw (ed.), The C.L.R. James Reader, (Oxford: Blackwell, 1992).
James C.L.R., 'Every Cook Can Govern: A Study of Democracy in Ancient Greece Its Meaning for Today', Correspondence, Vol. 2, No. 12. June 1956.
Korsch Karl, Marxism and Philosophy, (1923), (New York: Monthly Review Press, 1970).
Lebowitz Michael, Socialism for the 21st Century, (New York: Monthly Review Press, 2006).
Lenin Vladimir, 'Third All-Russia Congress of Soviets of Workers', Soldiers', and Peasants' Deputies', (1918), Pravda No. 9, No. 10 and No. 15, 1918.
Lenin Vladimir, What is to be Done?, (1902), (Moscow, Foreign Languages Publishing House, 1961).
Lenin Vladimir, The State and Revolution, (1917), (Petrograd: Zhizn I Znanie, 1918).
Lenin Vladimir, Imperialism: The Highest Stage of Capitalism, (1917), (Moscow: Progress Publishers, 1963).
Lenin Vladimir, 'Our Revolution', (1923), Pravda, No. 117, May 30, 1923.

Lukács Georg, History and Class Consciousness, (1923), (London: Merlin Press, 1967).
Lukács Georg, The Historical Novel, (1937), (Lincoln: University of Nebraska Press, 1983).
Luxemburg Rosa, The Crisis of German Social Democracy, (1916), (Zurich, February 1916).
Marx Karl and Friedrich Engels, The Communist Manifesto, (1848), (London: Verso, 2012).
Marx Karl, Economic and Philosophical Manuscripts of 1844, (1844), (Moscow: Progress Publishers, 1959).
Marx Karl, The German Ideology, (1845), (Moscow: Progress Publishers, 1968).
Marx Karl, Wage Labour and Capital, (1847), in Neue Rheinische Zeitung, April 5-8 and 11, 1849.
Marx Karl, The Eighteenth Brumaire of Louis Bonaparte, (1852), (Moscow: Progress Publishers, 1937).
Marx Karl, Speech at Anniversary of the People's Paper, (1856), (Moscow: Progress Publishers, 1969).
Marx Karl, Foundations of a Critique of Political Economy, (1857-1858).
Marx Karl, A Contribution to the Critique of Political Economy, (1859), (Moscow: Progress Publishers, 1970).
Marx Karl, Preface to a Contribution to the Critique of Political Economy, (1859), (Moscow: Progress Publishers, 1970).
Marx Karl, Capital Vol. I, (1867), (Moscow: Progress Publishers, 1965).
Marx Karl, Critique of the Gotha Programme, (1875), (Moscow: Progress Publishers, 1970).
Morris William, 'Art and Socialism', (1884), in A. L. Morton (ed.), Political Writings of William Morris, (London: Lawrence and Wishart, 1973).
Morris William, 'Letter on Socialism and Art', (1896), Justice, 7 March 1896.
Morris William, Signs of Change, (London: Longmans, Green, and Co, 1888).
Orwell George, Burmese Days, (New York: Harper Brothers, 1934).
Orwell George, Down and Out in Paris and London, (London: Victor Gollancz, 1933).
Orwell George, The Road to Wigan Pier, (London: Victor Gollancz, 1937).
Orwell George, Homage to Catalonia, (London: Secker and Warburg, 1938).
Orwell George, Animal Farm, (London: Secker and Warburg, 1945).
Orwell George, 'Why I Write', (1946), Gangrel, summer 1946.

Orwell George, Nineteen Eighty-Four, (London: Secker and Warburg, 1949).

Ostrovsky Nikolai, How the Steel Was Tempered, (1932-1934, 1936), (Moscow: Foreign Languages Publishing House, 1952).

Shelley Percy, Prometheus Unbound, A Lyrical Drama, in Four Acts, (1820), (London: C. and J. Ollier, 1820).

Sholokhov M.A., And Quietly Flows the Don, (New York: Alfred A. Knopf, 1934).

Thompson E.P., 'Socialism and the Intellectuals', (1957), Universities and Left Review, Volume 1, no 1, Spring 1957.

Thompson E.P., 'Socialist Humanism', (1957), The New Reasoner, No.1, Summer 1957, pp.105-143.

Tressell Robert, The Ragged-Trousered Philanthropists, (1914 and 1955), (London: Lawrence and Wishart, 1955).

Trotsky Leon, Literature and Revolution, (1924), (New York: Russell and Russell, 1957).

Trotsky Leon, Permanent Revolution, (1930), (Berlin: Left Opposition, 1930).

Williams Raymond, Culture and Society, (London: Chatto and Windus, 1958).

Williams, Raymond, 'Culture is Ordinary', (1958) in Raymond Williams, Resources of Hope: Culture, Democracy, and Socialism, (London: Verso, 1989), pp. 3-14.

Williams Raymond, The Long Revolution, (London: Chatto and Windus. 1961).

Williams Raymond, Marxism and Literature, (Oxford: Oxford University Press, 1977)